GUYANA AND ITS PEOPLE

Mini read chapters

ideal for diaspora members, travelers, history enthusiasts, and anyone eager to learn about Guyana and its people.

Unscripted
CHIC
2024

Introduction

Being Guyanese means belonging to a diverse
and multicultural society, primarily located
in the northern part of South America.
Guyana is characterized by its rich blend
of ethnic groups, including Indo-Guyanese,
Afro-Guyanese, Amerindians, and people
of mixed heritage. This diversity is reflected
in the country's cultural practices,
languages, and cuisine, where traditional
dishes like roti, curry, and pepperpot
are popular.

Guyana's natural beauty is another
significant aspect of its identity,
featuring lush rainforests, vast
savannas, and notable landmarks like
Kaieteur Falls. The people are known
for their warmth, resilience, and strong
community bonds. Celebrations like Diwali,
Christmas, and Mashramani (Guyana's
Republic Day) highlight the nation's cultural
richness and unity which this
book showcases.

Book Outline:

Chapter 1: Brief Historical Background
- Pre-Colonial Times: Amerindian heritage and societies
- Colonial Era: Dutch and British influence
- Independence and Modern History

Chapter 2: Ethnic Diversity
- Indo-Guyanese: Origins and cultural contributions
- Afro-Guyanese: Heritage and impact
- Amerindians: Traditions and lifestyle
- Other Ethnic Groups: Chinese, Portuguese, and Mixed heritage

Chapter 3: Cultural Practices
- Festivals and Celebrations: Diwali, Mashramani, Christmas, etc.
- Religious Diversity: Hinduism, Christianity, Islam, and Indigenous beliefs
- Traditional Music and Dance: Calypso, Soca, Chutney, and Folk dances

Chapter 4: Language and Communication
- Official Language: English
- Creole and Dialects: Unique expressions and slang
- Multilingualism: The role of Hindi, Urdu, and Indigenous languages

Chapter 5: Culinary Heritage
- Popular Dishes: Roti, curry, pepperpot, cook-up rice
- Influence of Different Ethnicities on Food
- Food and Social Gatherings

Chapter 6: Natural Beauty and Geography
- Major Landmarks: Kaieteur Falls, Rupununi Savannah, Shell Beach
- Biodiversity: Rainforests, wildlife, and conservation efforts
- Urban vs. Rural Life

Chapter 7: Social Structure and Community Life
- Family Dynamics and Values
- Education and Employment
- Role of Community and Diaspora

Chapter 8: Modern Challenges and Future Prospects
- Economic Development and Challenges
- Political Landscape
- Youth and Future Directions

Chapter 9: Some of the Highlights of Guyana

Chapter 1: Brief Historical Background

Guyana's history begins with its indigenous Amerindian tribes, including the Arawak, Carib, and Warao peoples, who lived sustainably off the land.

These tribes had rich cultural traditions, including unique languages, crafts, and spiritual practices.

Their way of life was deeply connected to the natural environment, which provided resources for their communities.

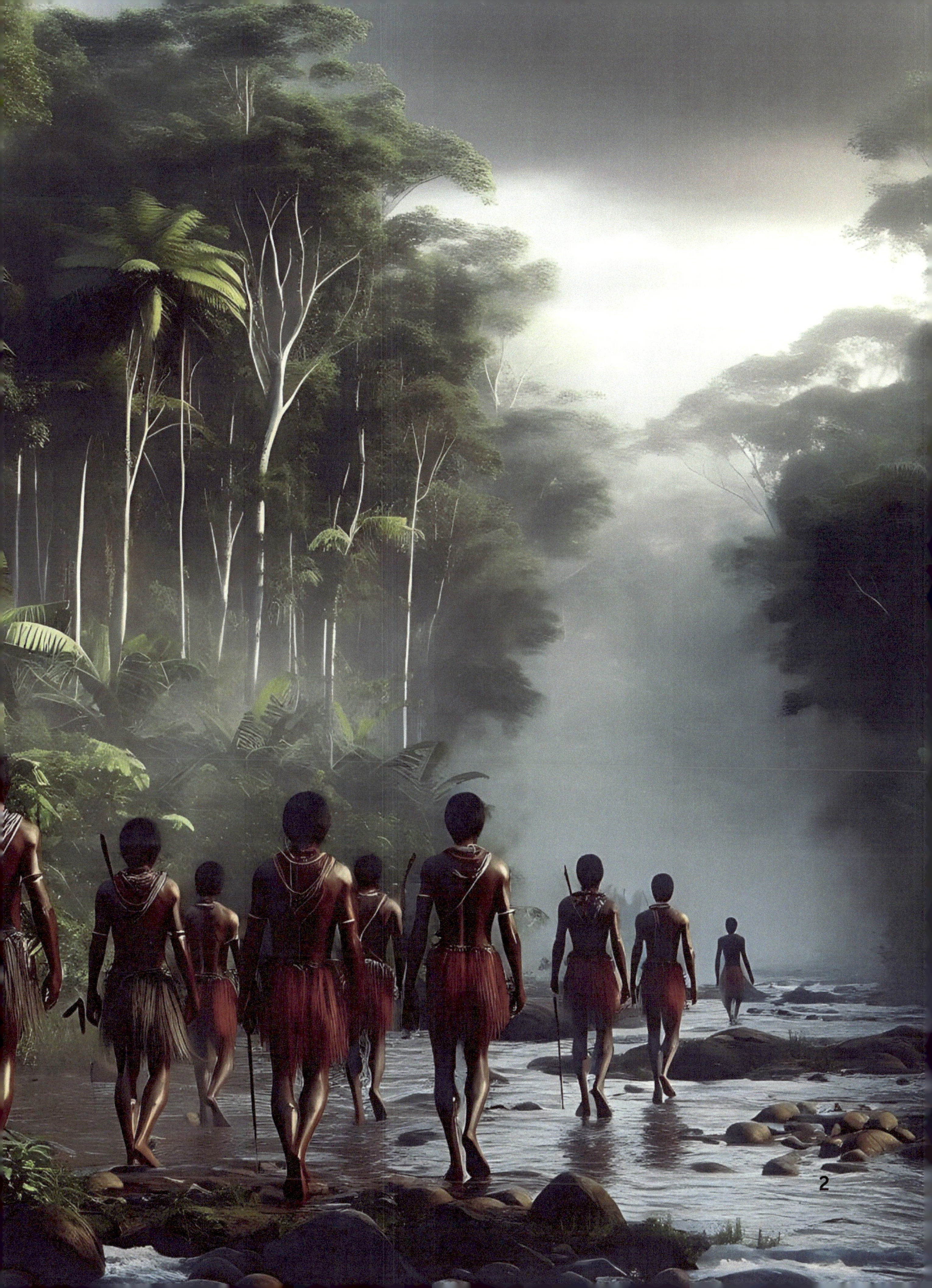

The Dutch were the first Europeans to establish settlements in Guyana in the early 17th century, building forts and trading posts along the coast.

In the 18th century, the British took control, shaping the colony's social and economic structures, including the establishment of sugar plantations worked by enslaved Africans.

This colonial period introduced significant cultural influences and laid the groundwork for Guyana's diverse population.

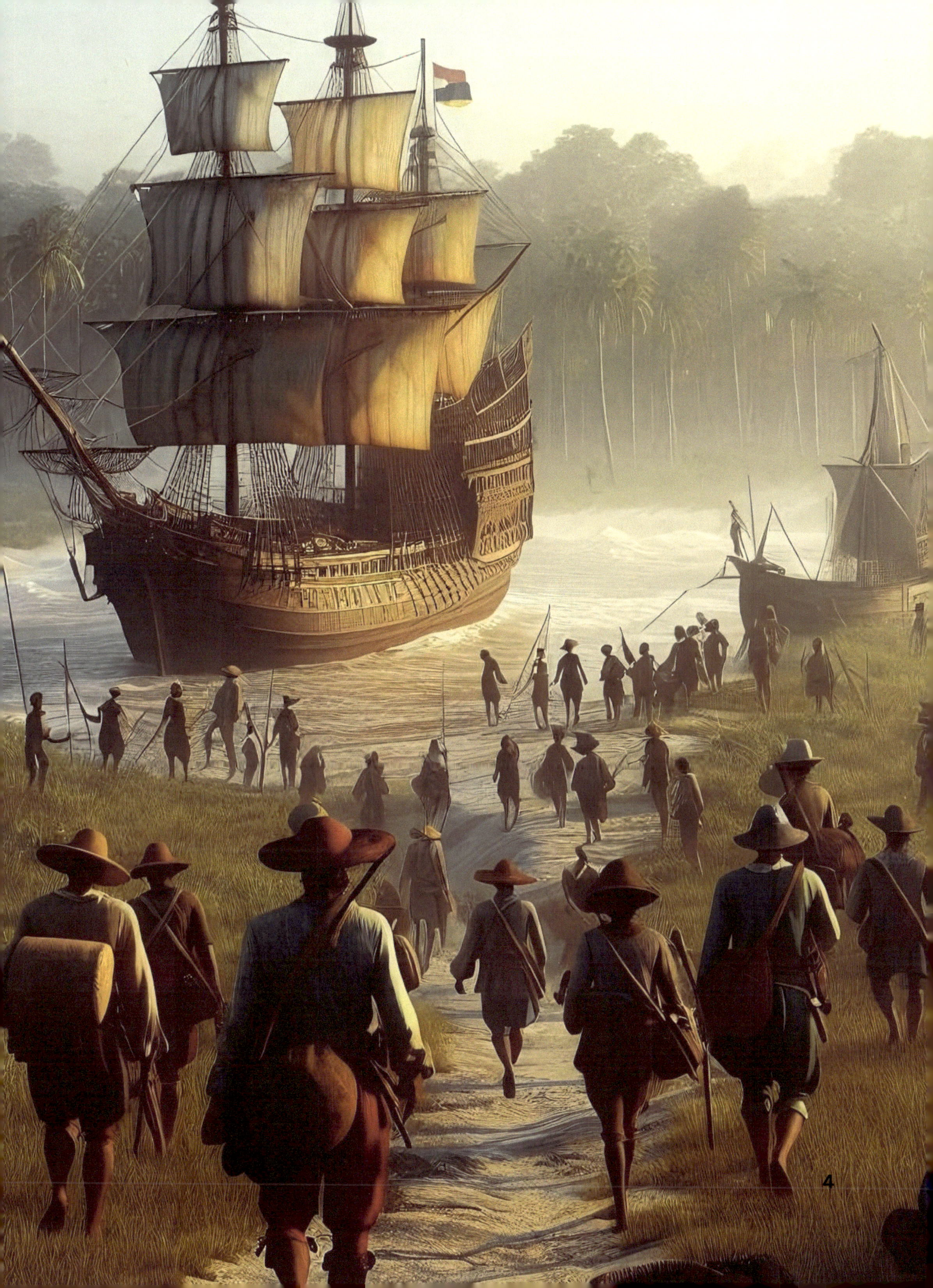

Guyana gained its independence from British rule on May 26, 1966, marking a significant milestone in its history.

The post-independence era saw the nation navigating political and economic challenges, striving to build a cohesive national identity.

Modern Guyana continues to evolve, balancing its rich cultural heritage with contemporary development and global integration.

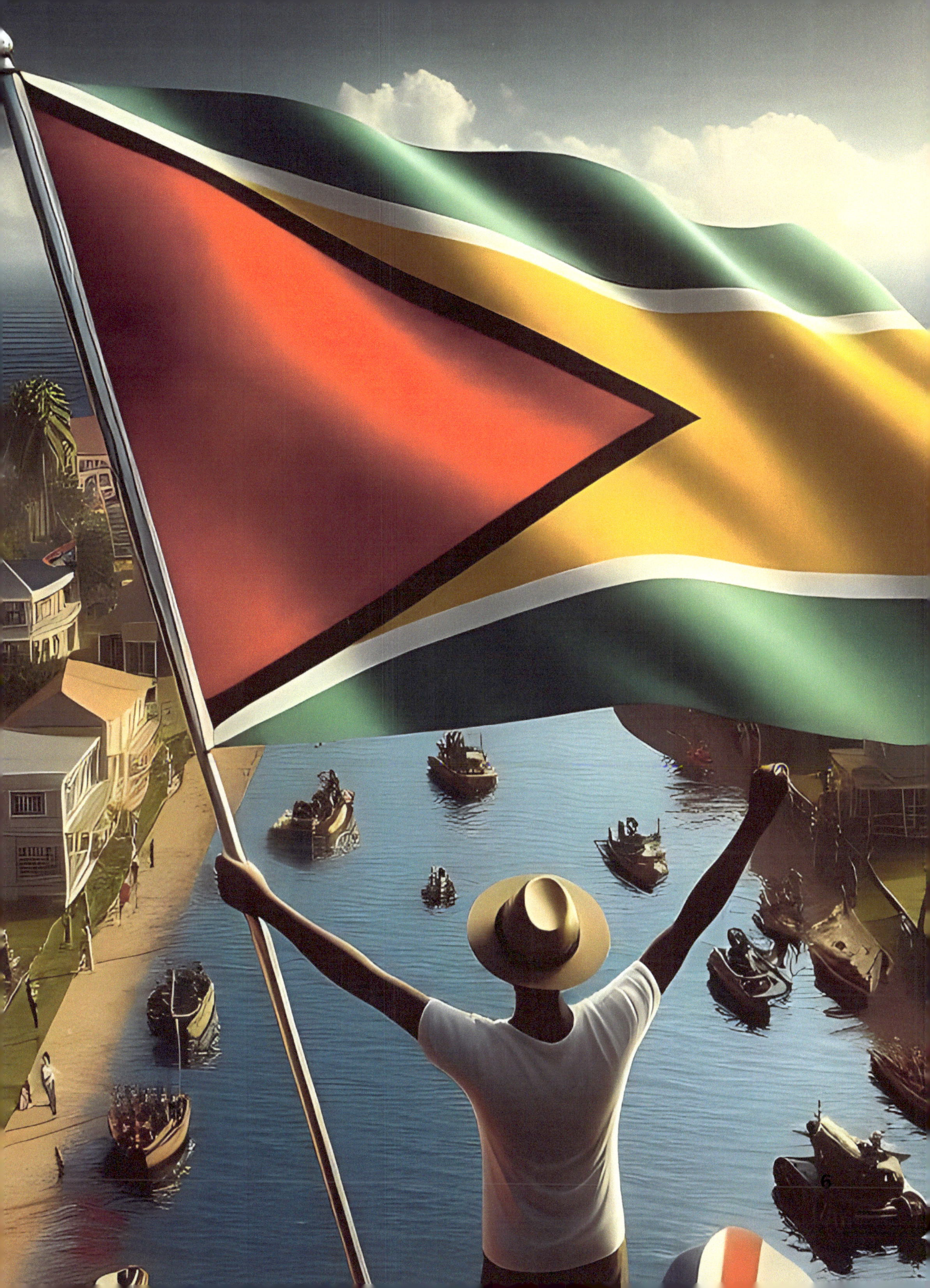

Chapter 2: Ethnic Diversity

The Indo-Guyanese community, primarily descendants of indentured laborers brought from India in the 19th century, forms a significant part of Guyana's population.

They have contributed richly to Guyanese culture, introducing traditions such as Diwali, colorful attire, and culinary delights like roti and curry.

Their influence extends to various sectors, including politics, business, and the arts, enriching the nation's multicultural fabric.

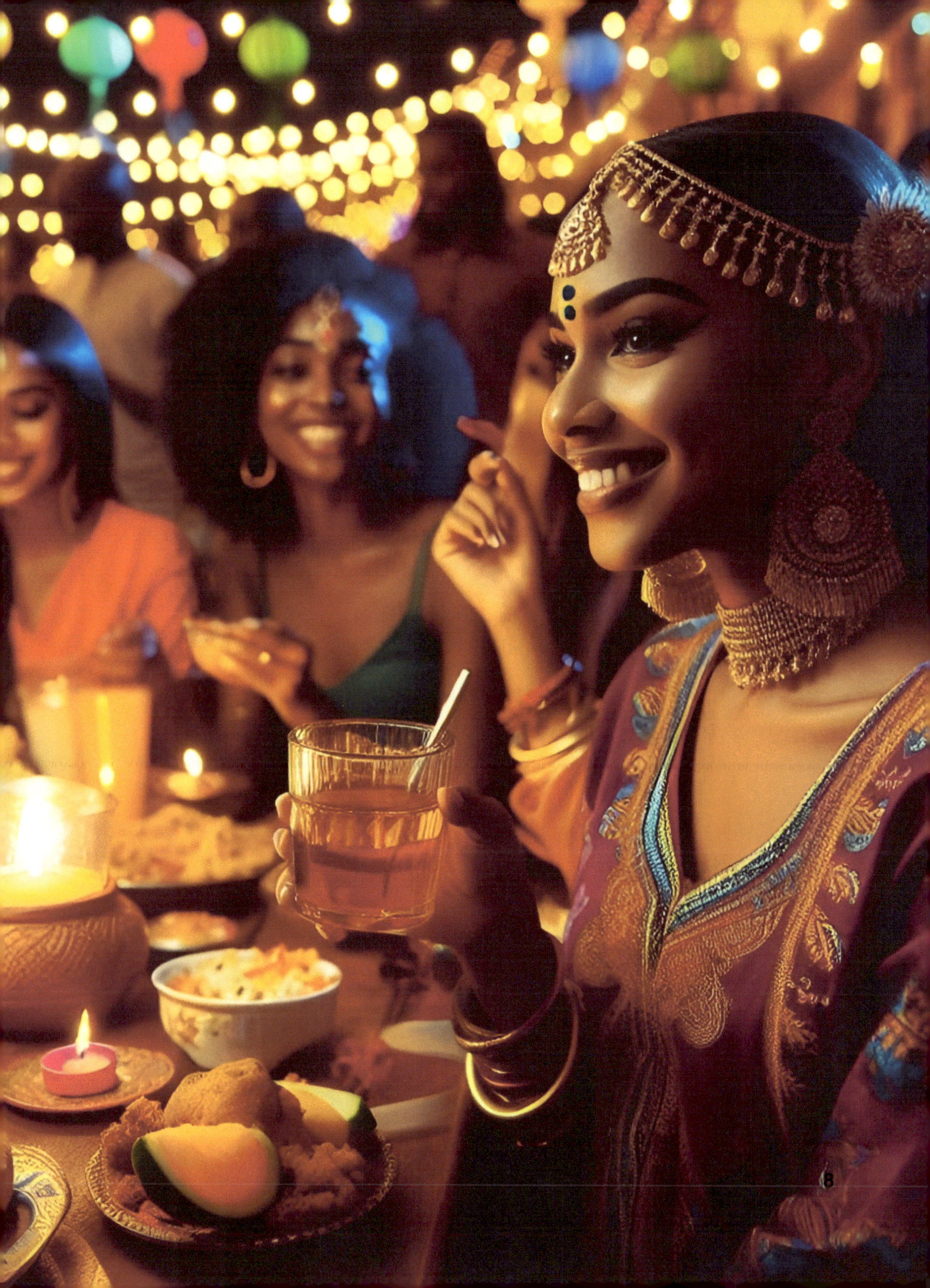

The Afro-Guyanese community, descendants of enslaved Africans brought to Guyana during the colonial era, have profoundly shaped the nation's cultural and social dynamics.

They have contributed vibrant traditions such as the celebration of emancipation, spiritual practices like Jonkonnu, and influential musical genres like reggae and soca.

Afro-Guyanese culture reflects resilience, creativity, and a strong sense of identity rooted in their historical experiences and struggles.

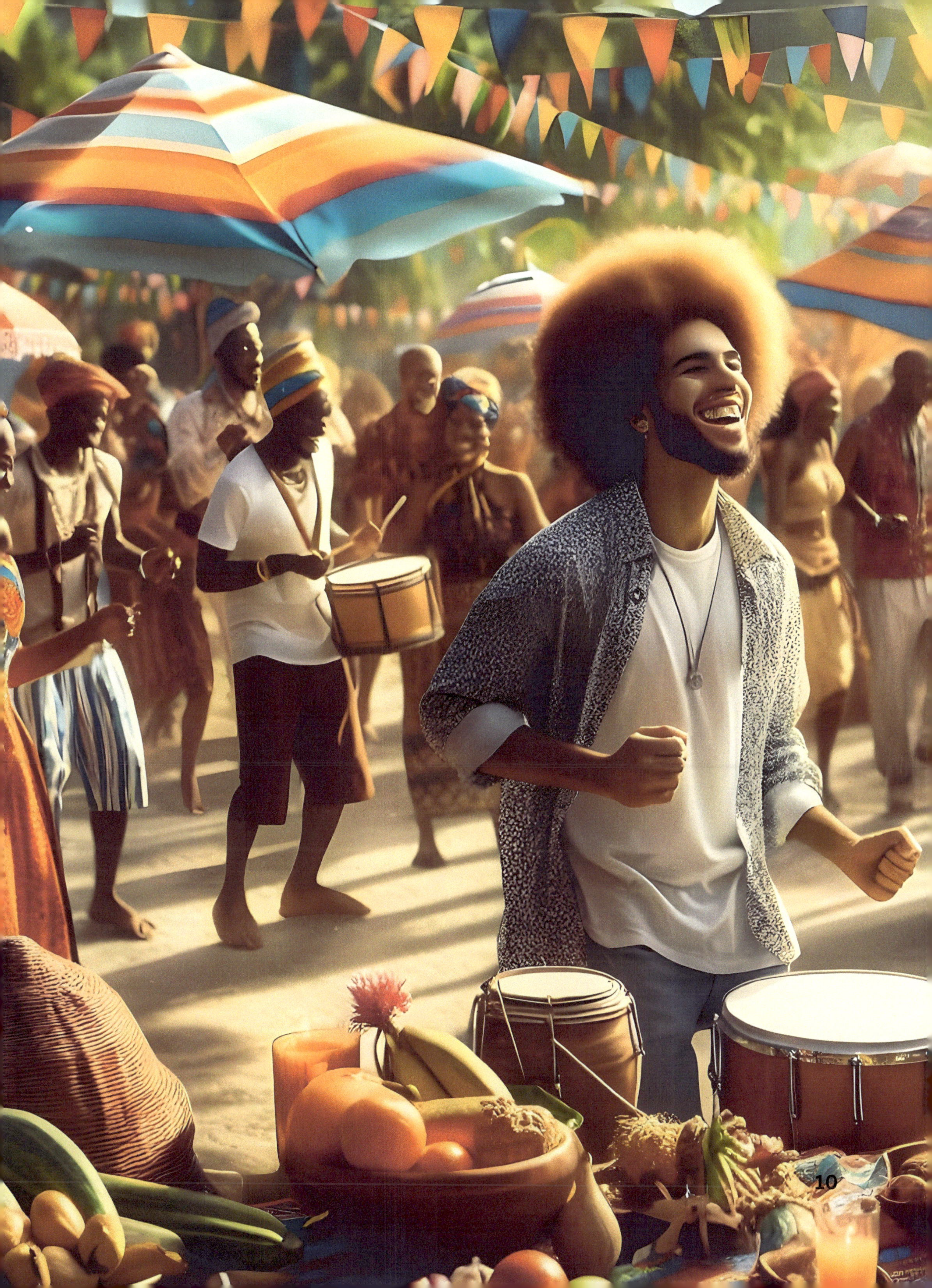

The Amerindian communities of Guyana, comprising several distinct tribes such as the Arawak, Carib, and Warao, maintain rich cultural traditions deeply connected to the land.

Their heritage includes intricate crafts, spiritual beliefs centered on nature, and communal practices that emphasize harmony with the environment.

Despite challenges like land rights issues and modernization, Amerindian cultures continue to play a vital role in preserving Guyana's diverse cultural tapestry.

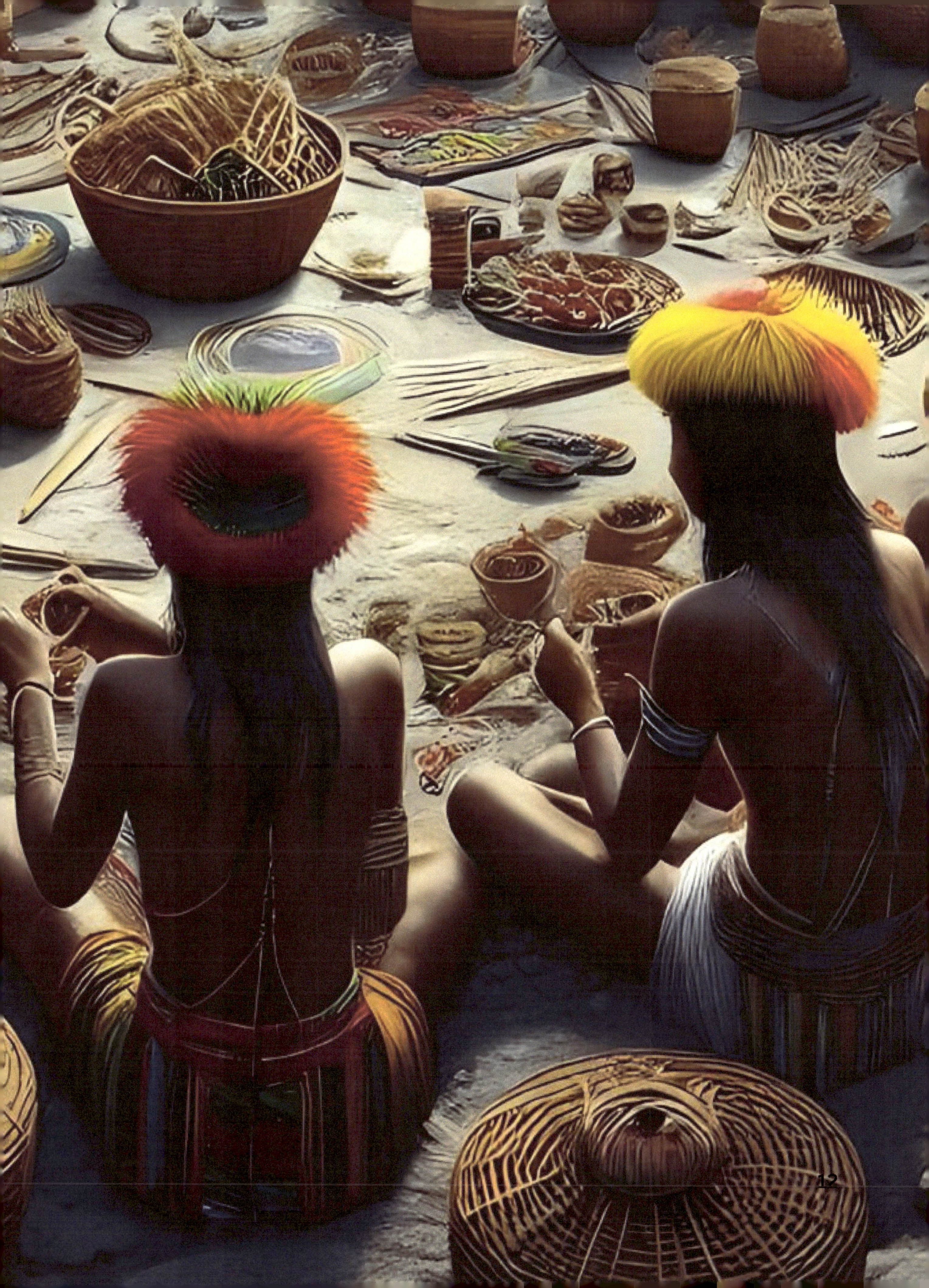

Other ethnic groups in Guyana, such as the Chinese, Portuguese, and those of mixed heritage, contribute unique perspectives and traditions to the country's multicultural mosaic.

The Chinese community, for instance, has left a lasting impact through their cuisine and cultural festivals like Chinese New Year.

Portuguese influences are evident in aspects of Guyanese cuisine and Catholic religious practices, enriching the cultural diversity of the nation.

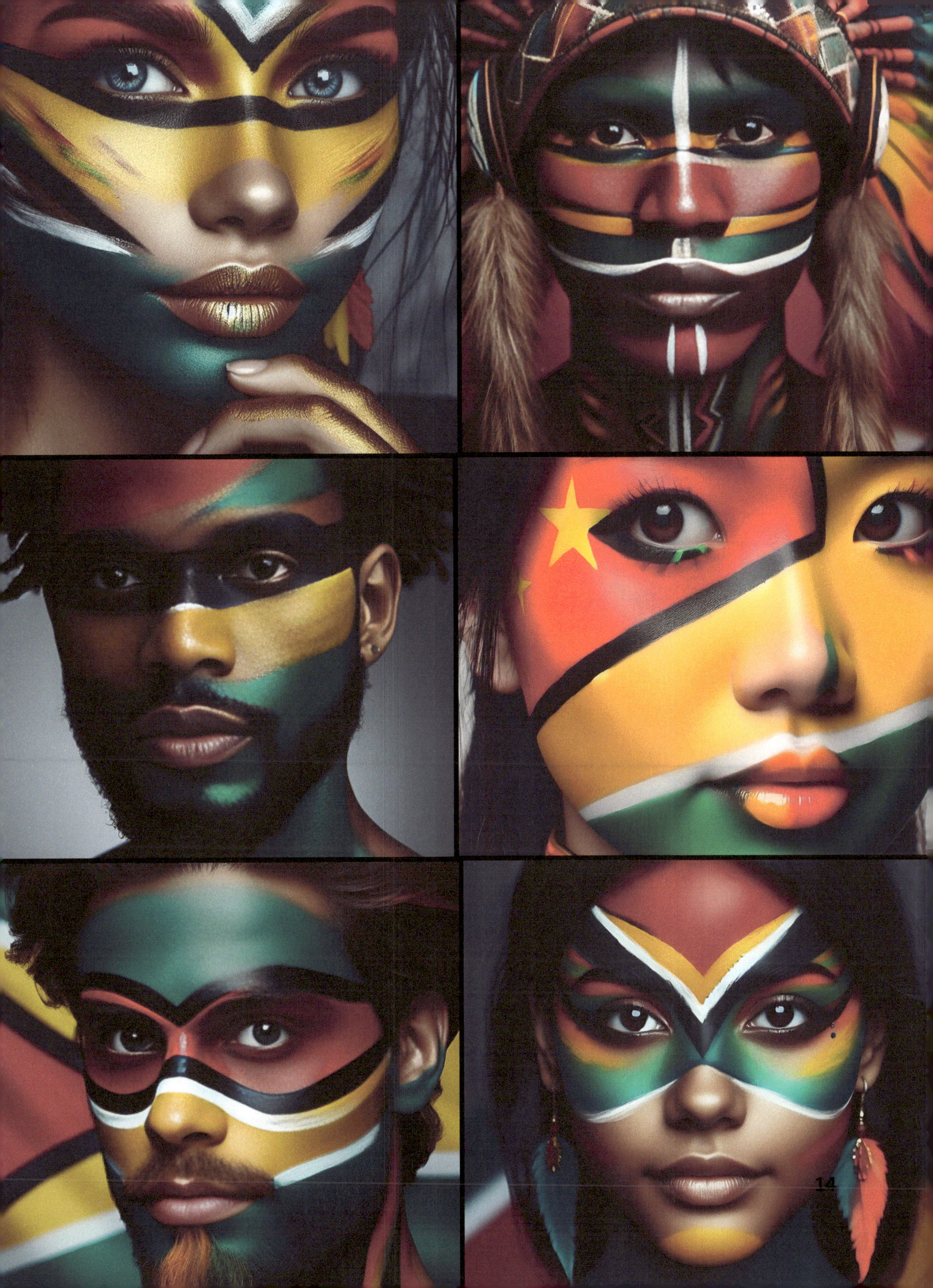

Chapter 3: Cultural Practices

Festivals and celebrations are integral to Guyanese cultural life, reflecting the country's diverse ethnic and religious communities.

Diwali, celebrated by the Indo-Guyanese community, lights up homes and streets with diyas (oil lamps) symbolizing the triumph of light over darkness.

Mashramani, originating from the Amerindian word for celebration, marks Guyana's Republic Day with vibrant parades, music, and dancing, showcasing the nation's unity and cultural pride.

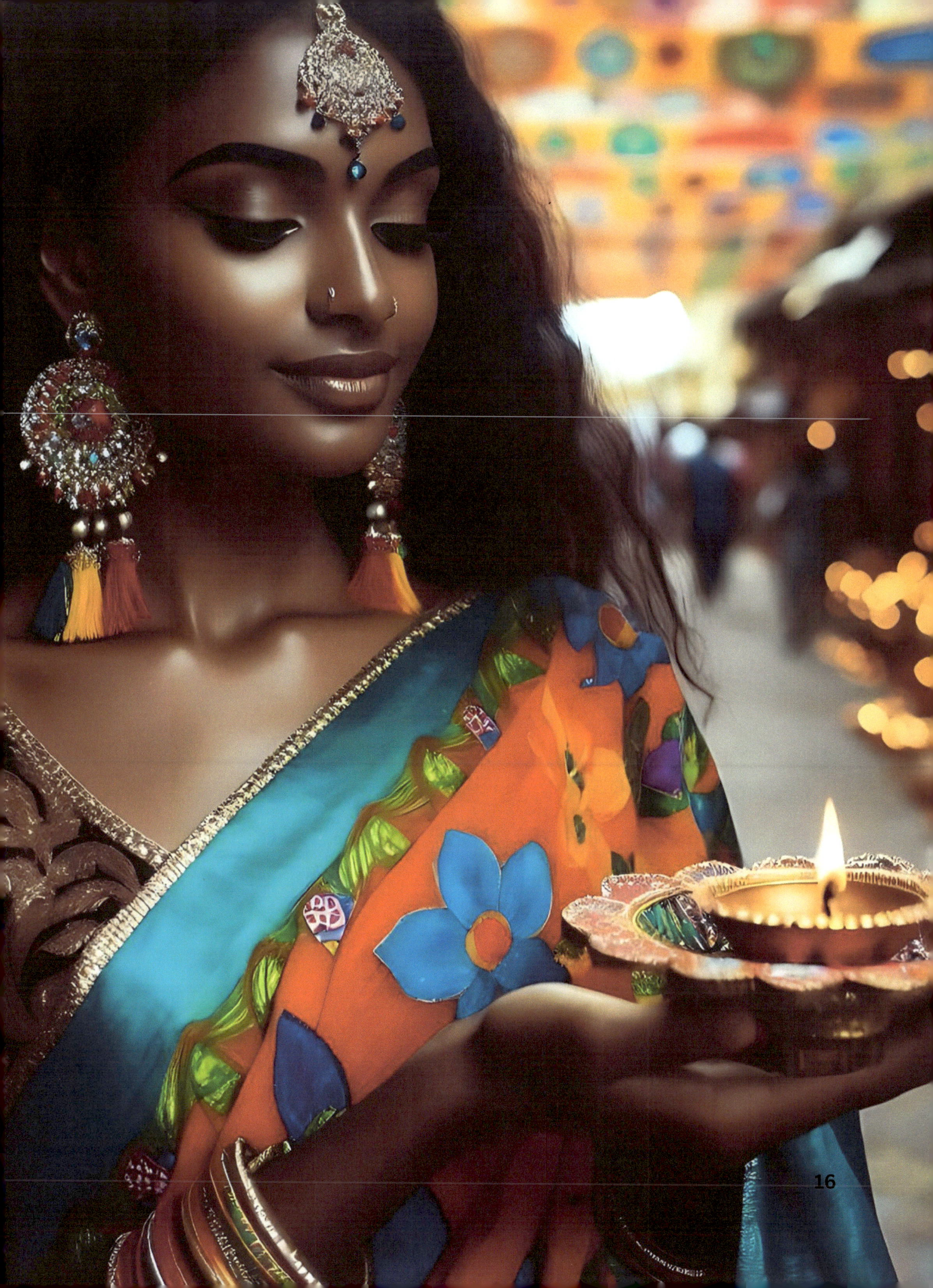

Religious diversity in Guyana is prominently represented by Hinduism, Christianity, Islam, and traditional Indigenous beliefs.

Hindu temples dot the landscape, hosting elaborate ceremonies and rituals during festivals like Phagwah (Holi) and Divali (Diwali).

Christian denominations, including Anglican, Roman Catholic, and Pentecostal, play a significant role in the social and cultural life of the nation, with churches serving as community hubs for worship and outreach.

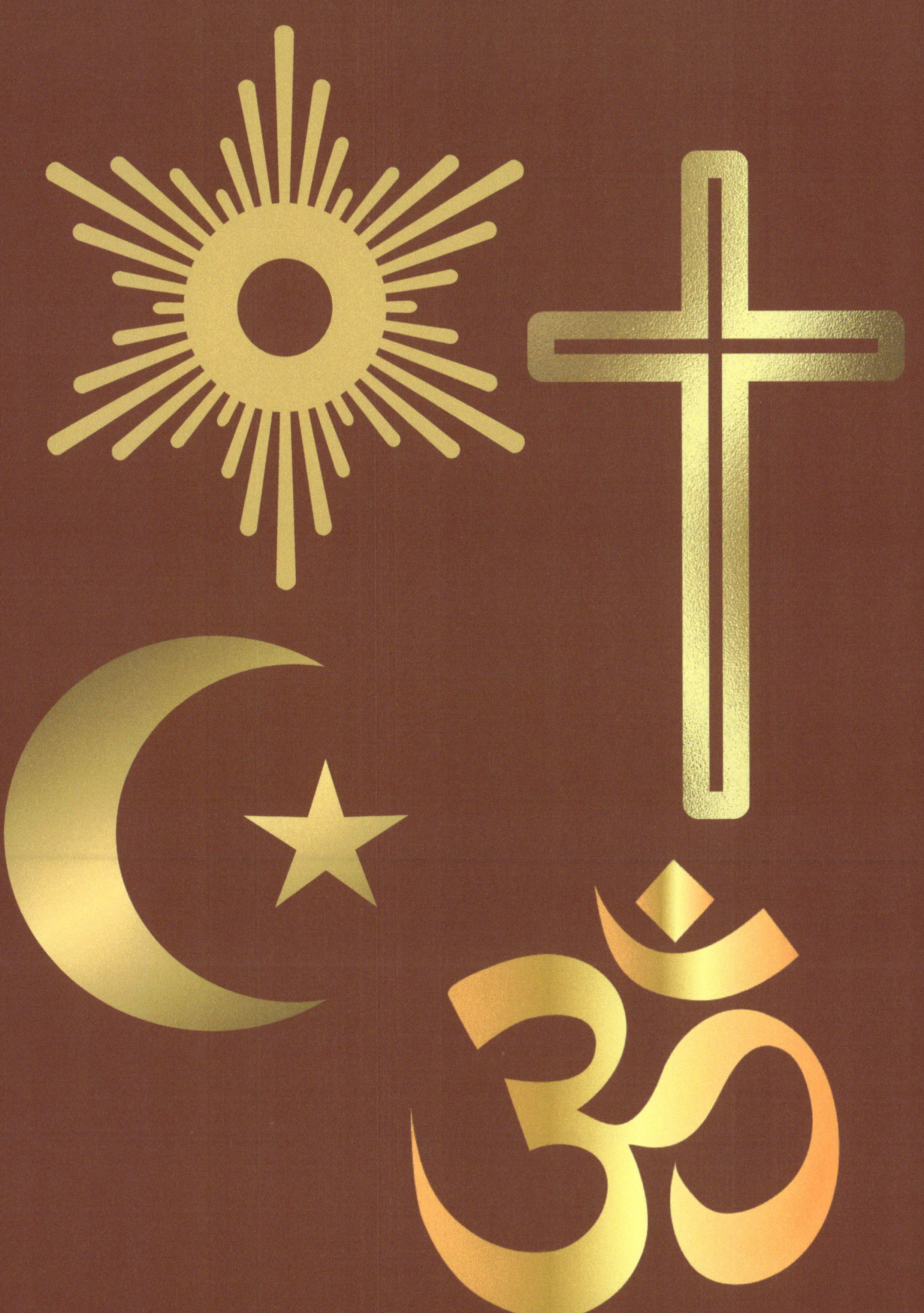

Traditional music and dance in Guyana encompass a vibrant spectrum of styles rooted in its diverse cultural heritage.

Calypso and Soca music, influenced by Afro-Guyanese rhythms, are popular during festivals and celebrations like Mashramani.

Chutney music, blending Indian and Caribbean influences, has gained widespread popularity, reflecting the fusion of Indo-Guyanese culture with local musical traditions.

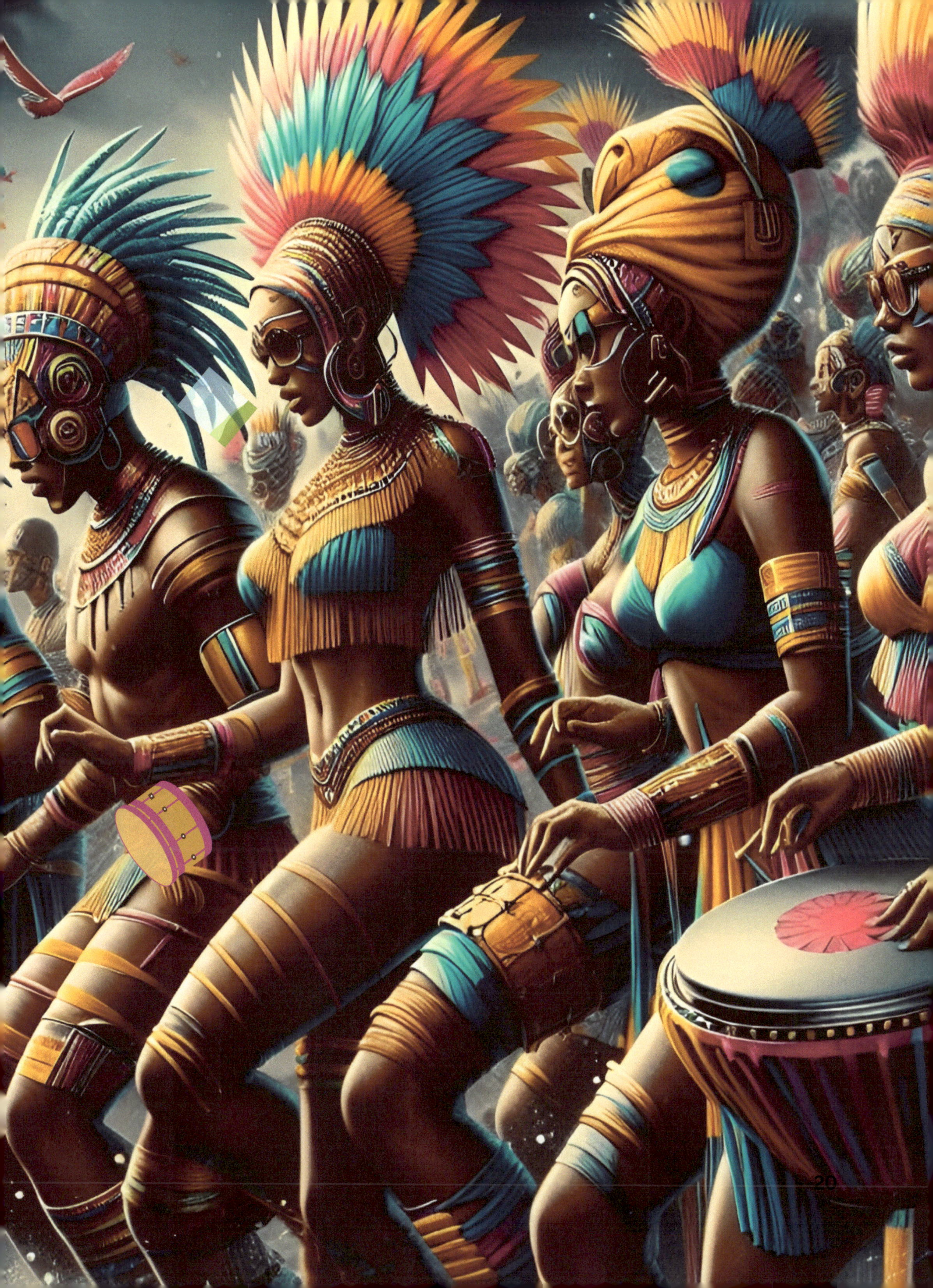

Chapter 4: Language and Communication

English serves as the official language of Guyana, used in government, education, and business sectors throughout the country.

However, Guyanese Creole, also known as Guyanese English Creole or "Creolese," is widely spoken among locals in everyday interactions, adding a distinct flavor to communication.

Creolese incorporates elements from English, African languages, and various other linguistic influences, reflecting the country's multicultural heritage.

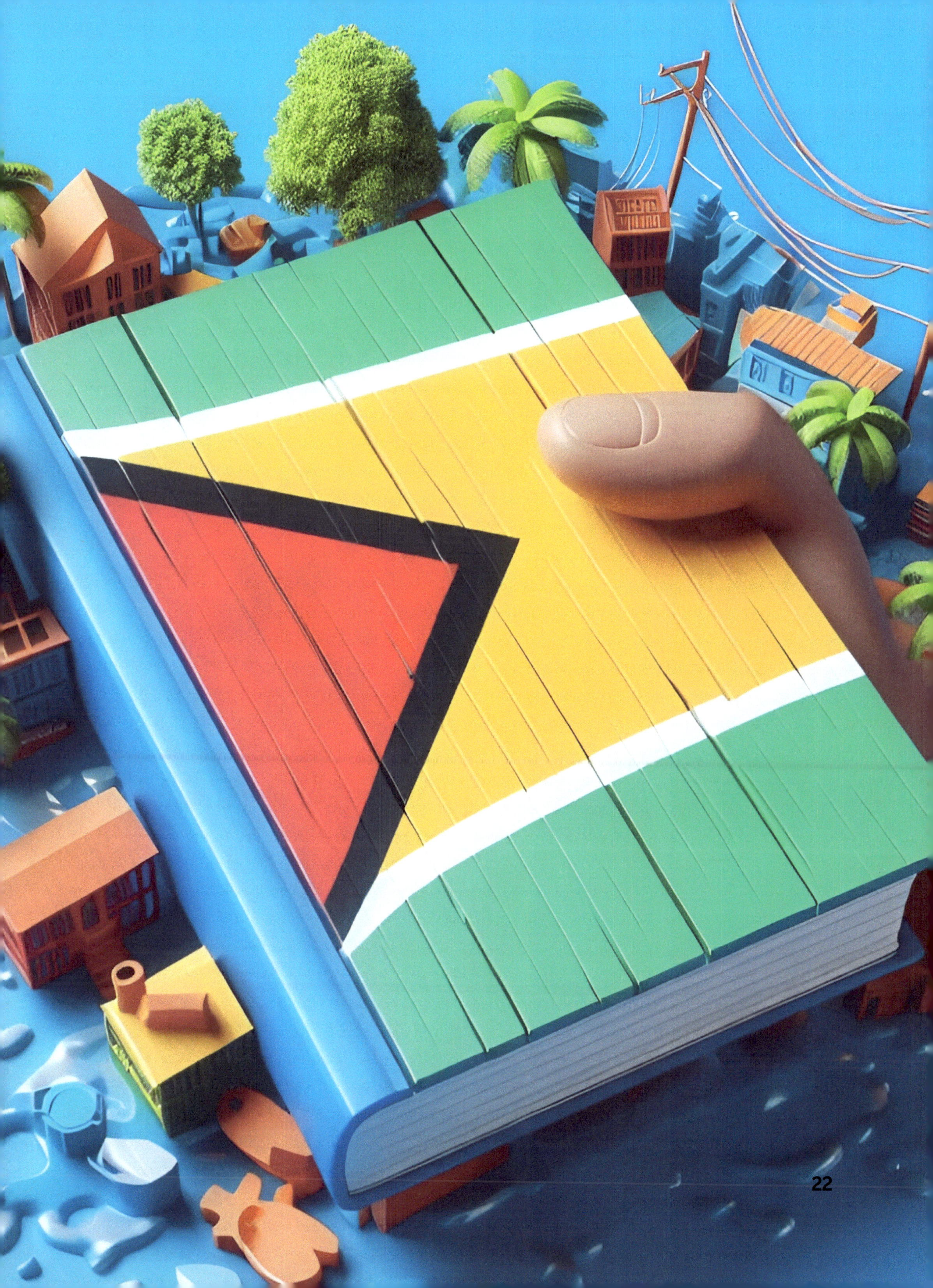

Guyana's linguistic landscape is enriched by the presence of Hindi, Urdu, and Indigenous languages, each playing significant roles in different aspects of daily life.

Hindi and Urdu are predominantly spoken among the Indo-Guyanese community, preserving cultural identity through language, literature, and religious texts.

Indigenous languages, such as Arawak and Carib, although less widely spoken today, continue to carry ancestral knowledge and traditions, contributing to the nation's linguistic diversity.

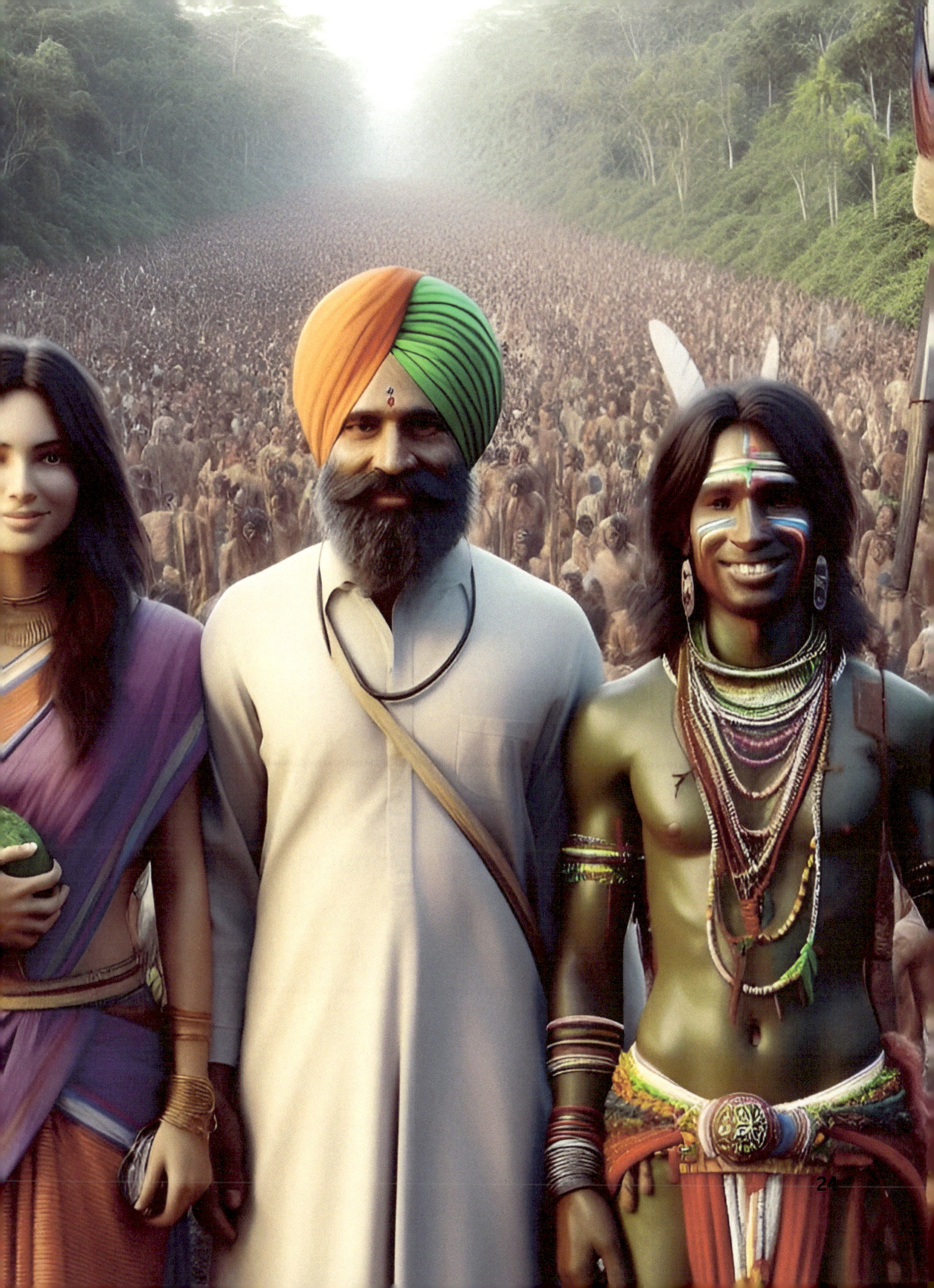

Guyanese society exhibits a remarkable level of multilingualism, where individuals often switch effortlessly between languages depending on social contexts.

This linguistic flexibility fosters a sense of cultural inclusivity and unity among diverse ethnic groups.

Moreover, the ability to navigate multiple languages enhances communication across different sectors, contributing to a cohesive national identity.

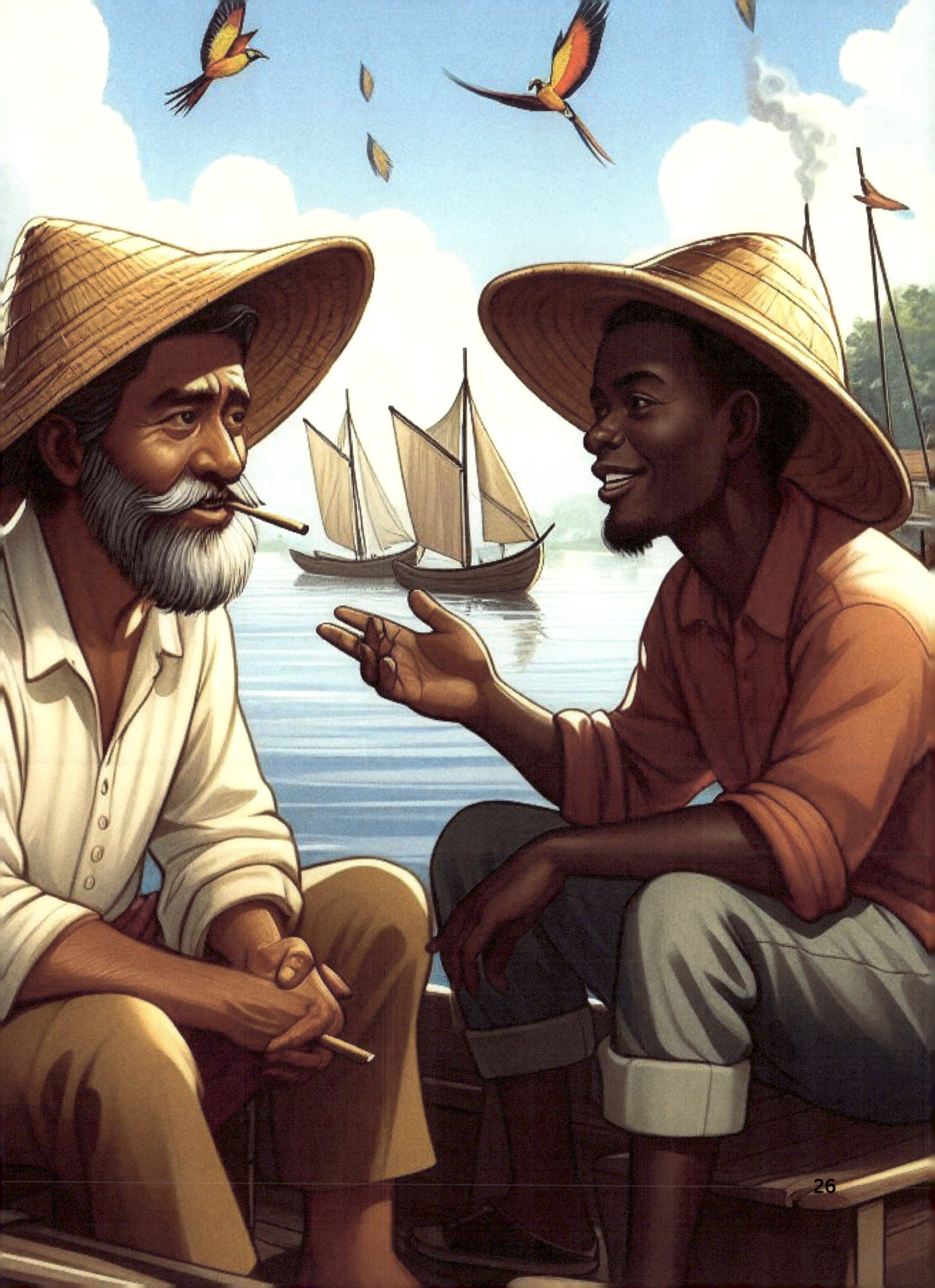

Chapter 5: Culinary Heritage

Guyanese cuisine is a rich tapestry of flavors influenced by the country's diverse ethnic groups and cultural heritage.

Staple dishes like roti, curry, and pepperpot reflect the fusion of Indian, African, and Indigenous culinary traditions.

The use of aromatic spices and fresh ingredients characterizes Guyanese cooking, creating dishes that are both hearty and flavorful.

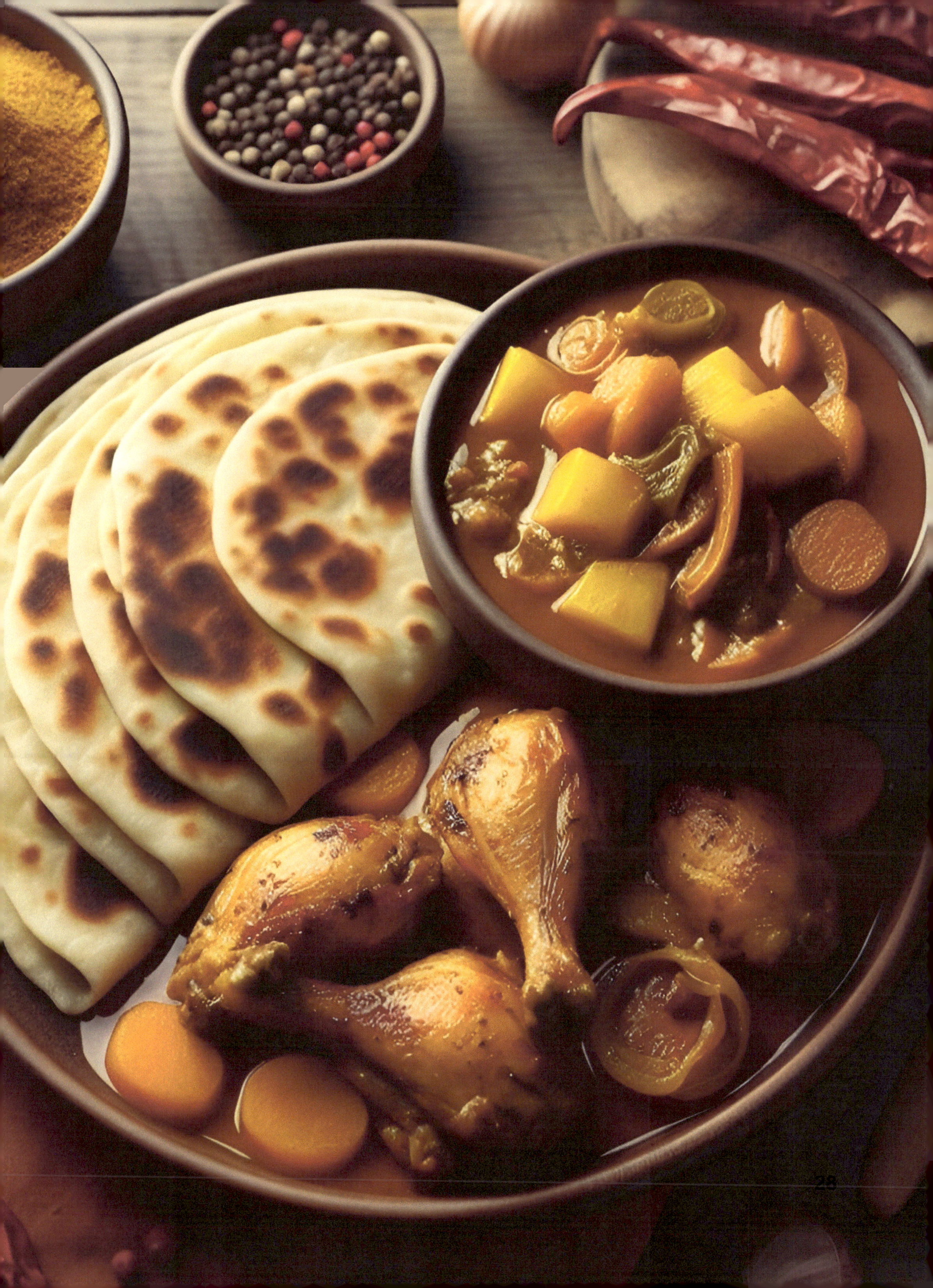

Guyanese cuisine is a vibrant tapestry woven from the culinary traditions of its diverse ethnic communities.

 From fiery curries and savory rotis brought by the Indo-Guyanese, to hearty pepperpot stew from the Afro-Guyanese, each dish tells a story of cultural fusion and adaptation.

These foods not only nourish the body but also serve as a connection to ancestral roots and a celebration of Guyana's multicultural identity.

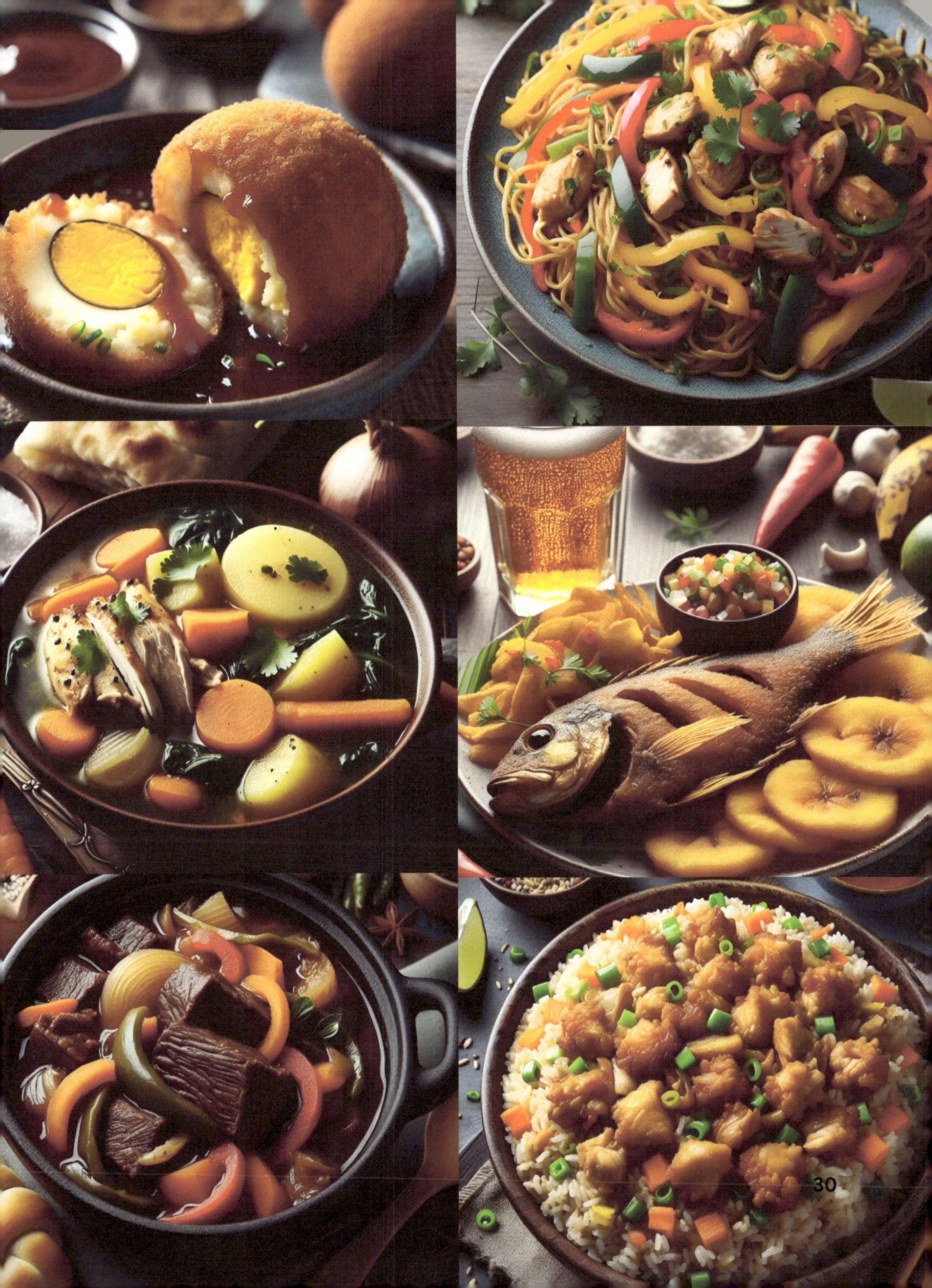

Food plays a central role in social gatherings and celebrations across Guyana, where meals are occasions for community bonding and cultural exchange.

Festivals like Phagwah (Holi), Mashramani, and Christmas are marked by feasts featuring traditional dishes shared among family and friends.

The preparation and sharing of food symbolize hospitality and unity, embodying the warmth and generosity of Guyanese culture.

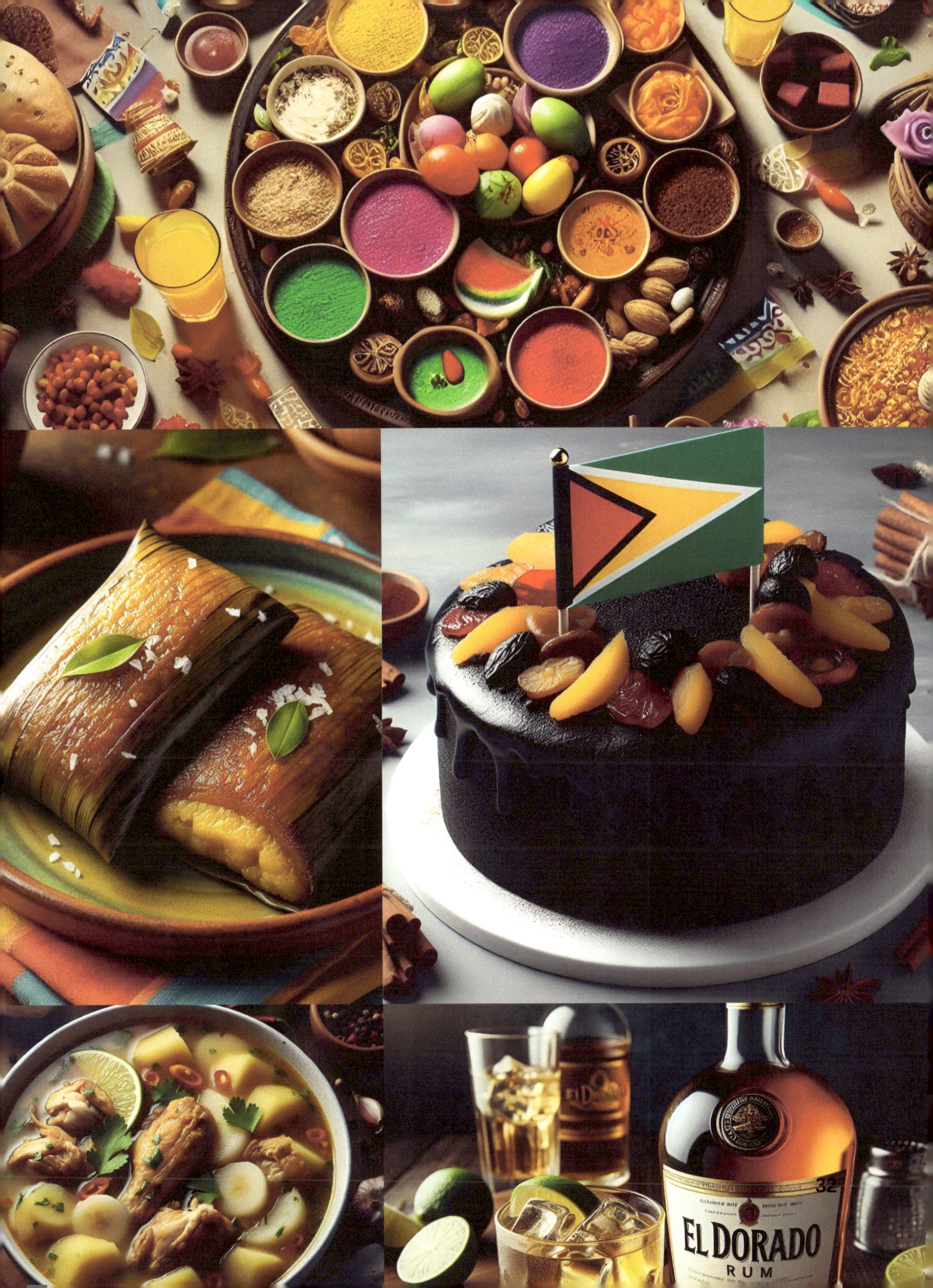

EL DORADO
RUM

Chapter 6: Natural Beauty and Geography

Guyana's natural beauty is characterized by its diverse landscapes, including expansive rainforests teeming with biodiversity.

The country boasts iconic landmarks such as Kaieteur Falls, one of the world's largest single-drop waterfalls, drawing visitors from around the globe.

 Its pristine environments, from the Rupununi savannahs to the untouched interior, showcase the ecological richness that defines Guyana.

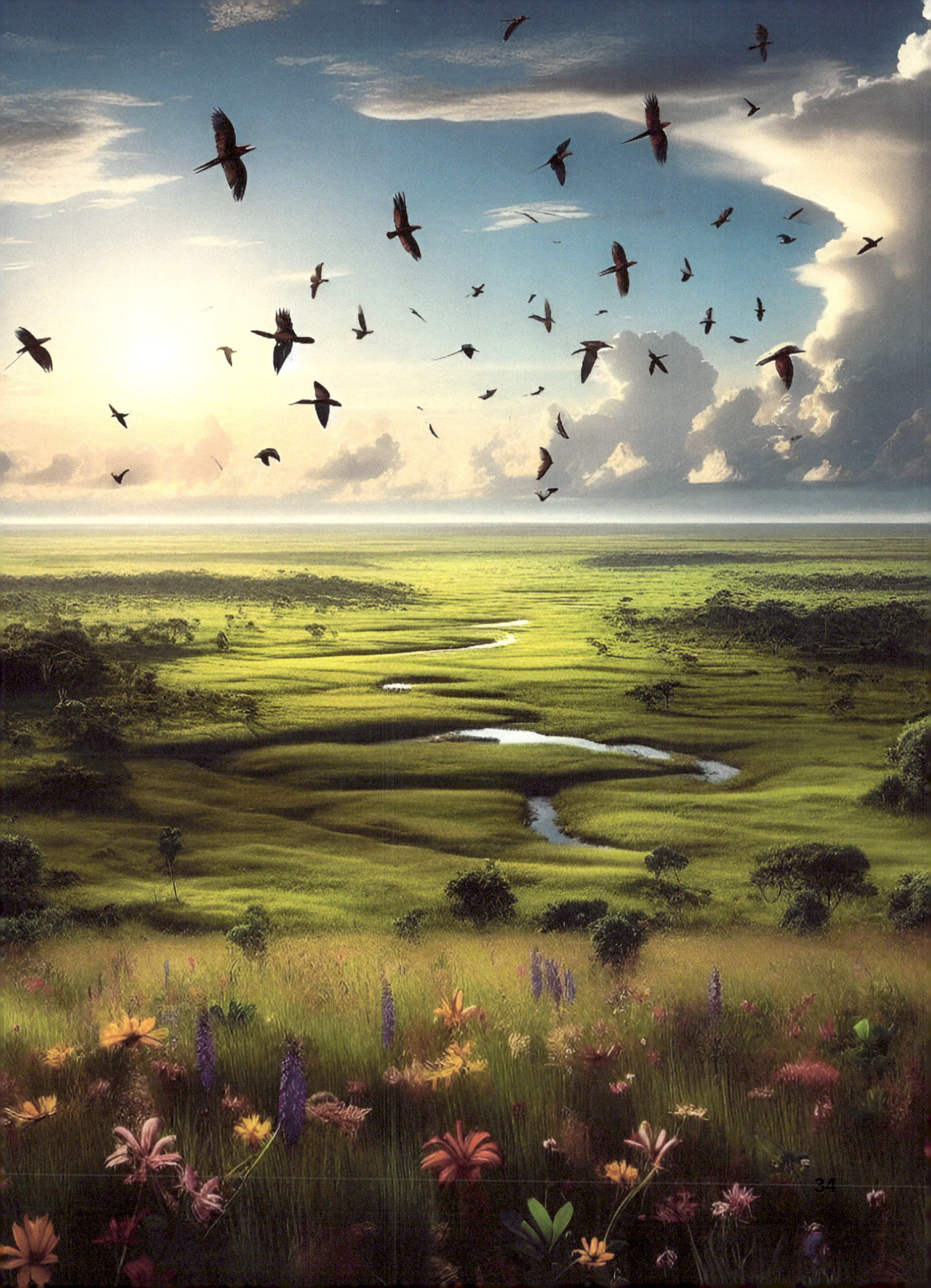

Guyana's biodiversity is showcased through its rich array of wildlife, including jaguars, giant river otters, and numerous bird species like the Harpy Eagle.

Conservation efforts are crucial in protecting these habitats, with initiatives focusing on sustainable practices and eco-tourism.

The country's commitment to preserving its natural heritage ensures future generations can continue to appreciate its biological diversity and pristine landscapes.

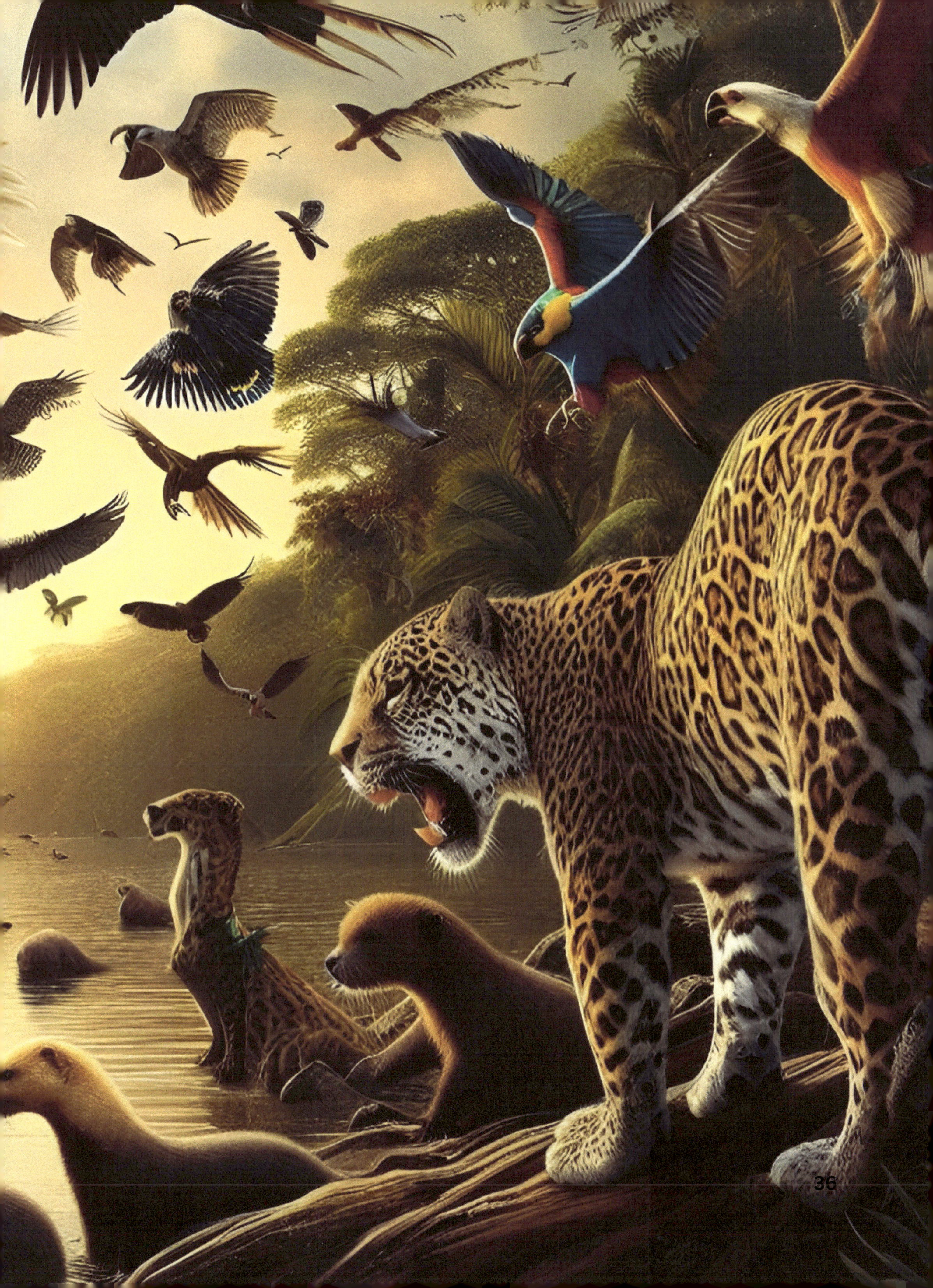

Urban centers like Georgetown contrast with rural areas, offering bustling markets, colonial architecture, and vibrant cultural scenes.

Rural life in Guyana often revolves around agriculture, with communities cultivating crops like rice, sugar cane, and vegetables.

Despite modernization, rural areas maintain a strong connection to traditional practices and communal lifestyles, reflecting a blend of old and new in Guyanese society.

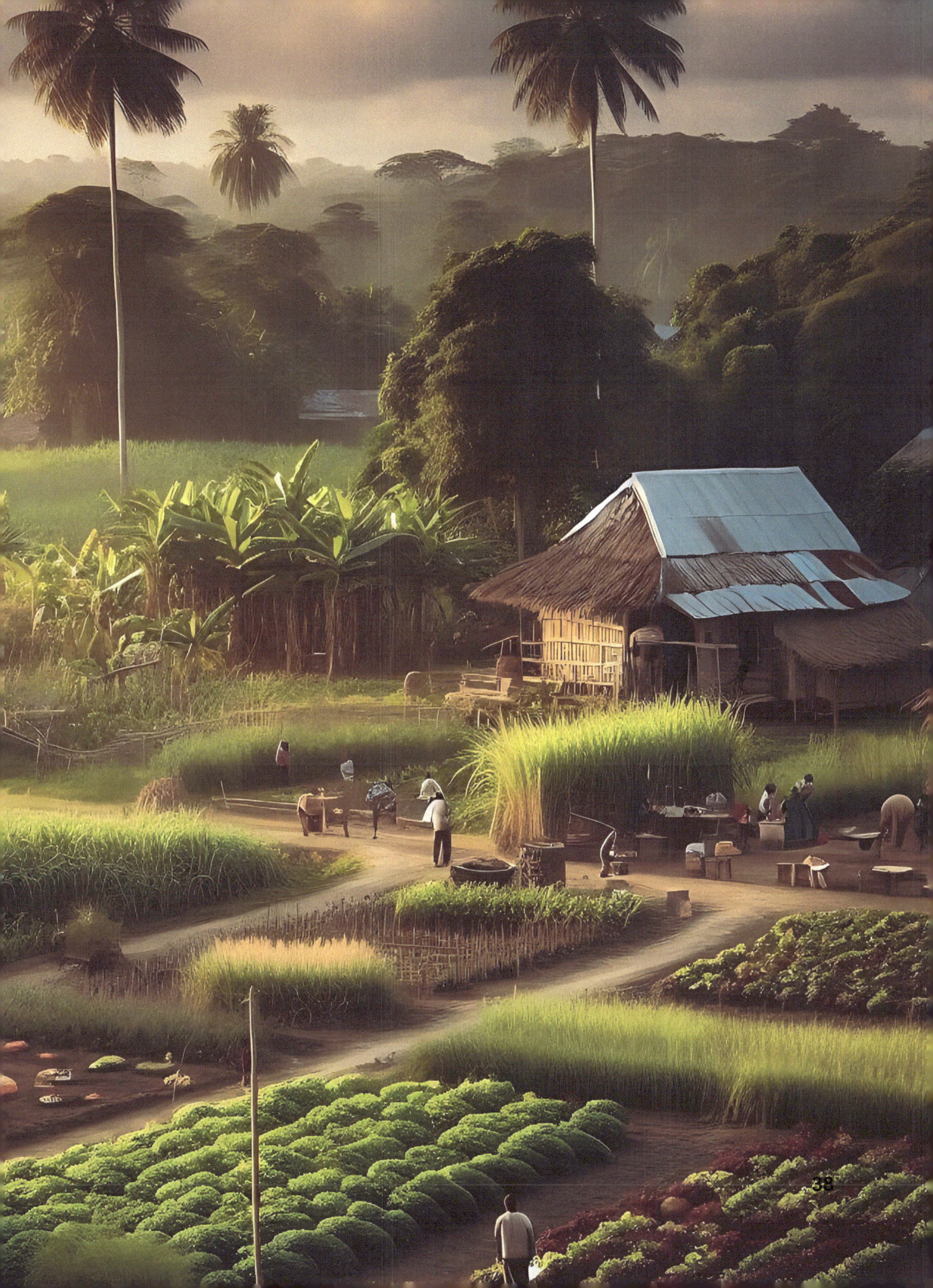

Chapter 7: Social Structure and Community Life

Family forms the cornerstone of Guyanese society, with strong bonds and collective support networks prevailing across generations.

Extended families often live together or close by, fostering a sense of unity and shared responsibility.

These familial ties play a crucial role in social and economic life, providing a safety net and cultural continuity within communities.

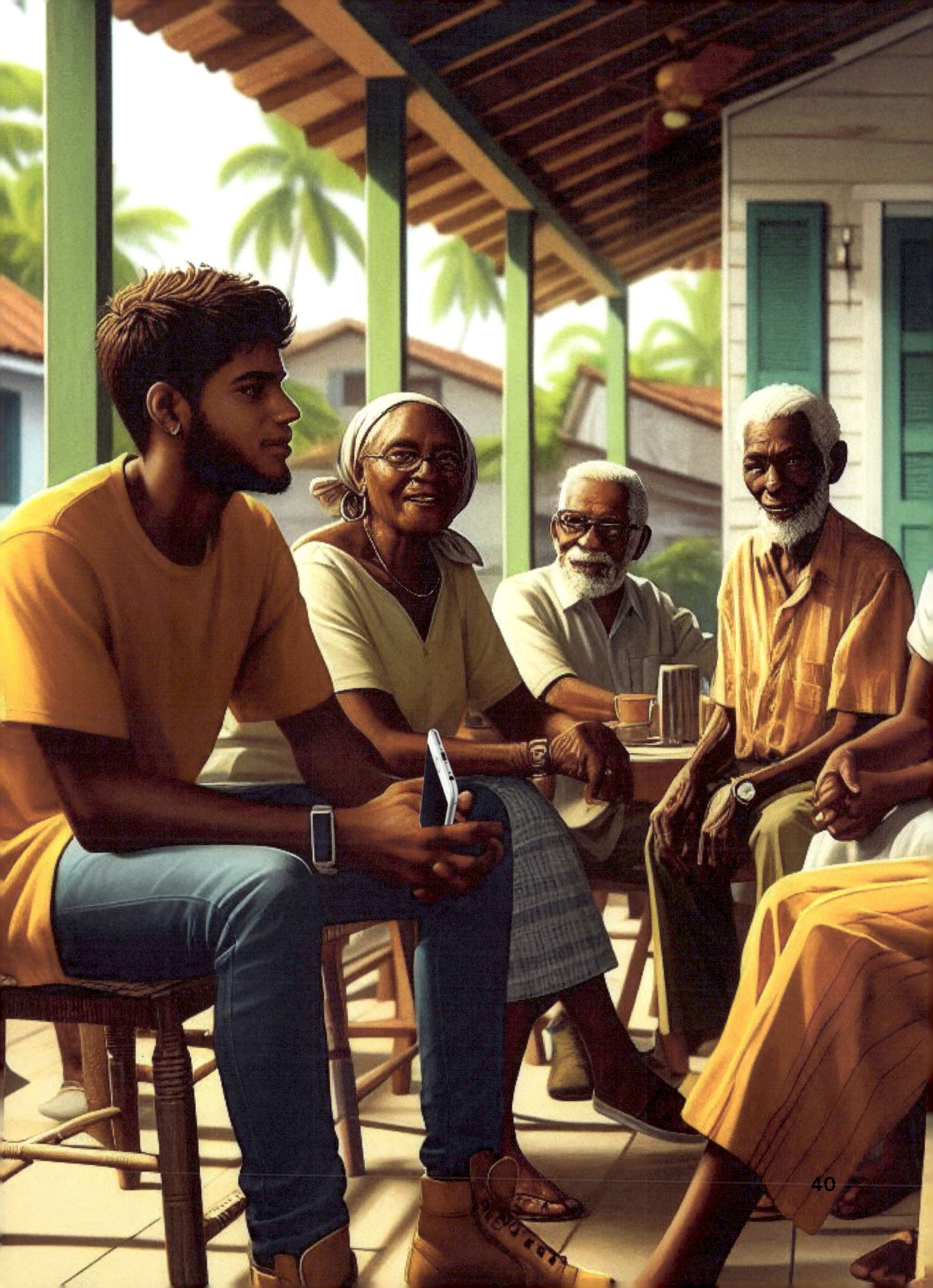

Education in Guyana is considered a vital pathway to social mobility and personal advancement, with a focus on achieving higher levels of literacy and skills development.

The education system includes both public and private institutions, with efforts to improve access and quality across the country.

Schools play a central role in shaping young minds and preparing them for future opportunities in a rapidly changing global landscape.

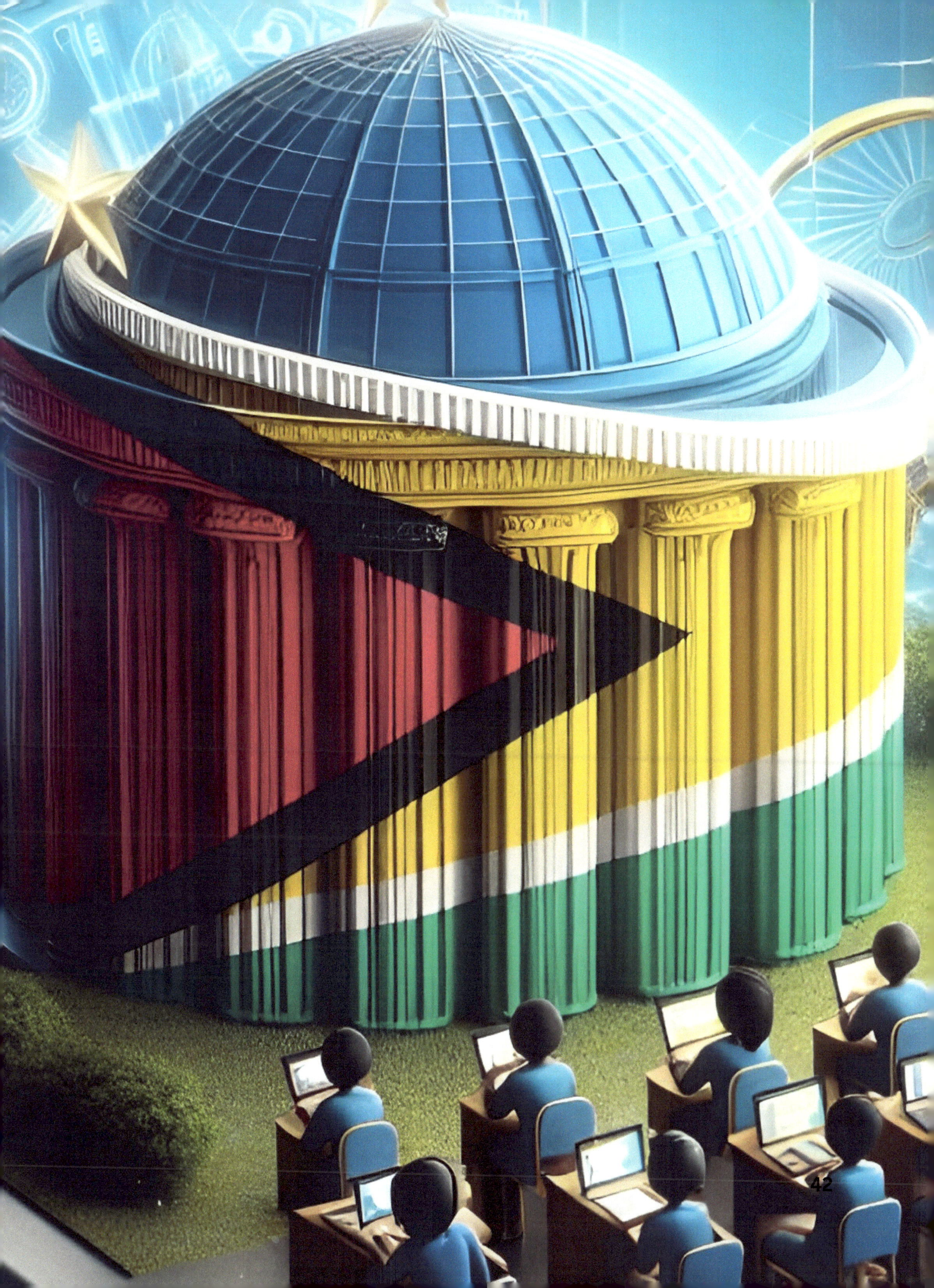

Community plays a pivotal role in the daily lives of Guyanese people, providing a support network and fostering a sense of belonging.

Social gatherings, such as religious ceremonies, cultural festivals, and community events, strengthen these bonds and celebrate shared heritage.

Through collective efforts and mutual aid, communities in Guyana uphold traditions, tackle challenges, and promote unity amidst cultural diversity.

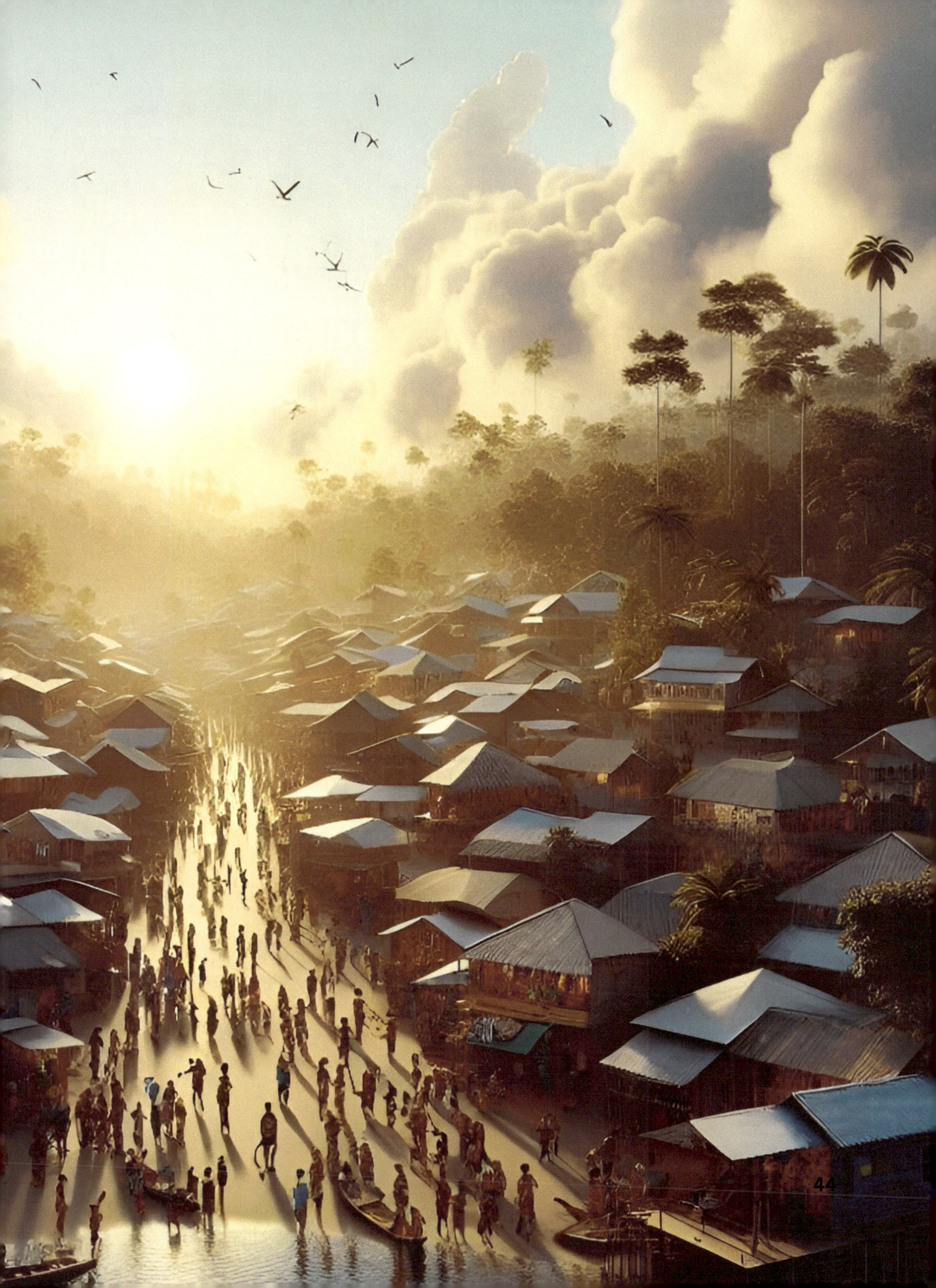

44

Chapter 8: Modern Challenges and Future Prospects

Modern Guyana faces economic challenges despite its rich natural resources, including gold, timber, and bauxite.

Issues such as income inequality, infrastructure development, and unemployment require sustainable solutions to promote inclusive growth.

The government and private sectors are actively working to diversify the economy beyond traditional sectors, aiming to foster innovation and attract foreign investment for long-term prosperity.

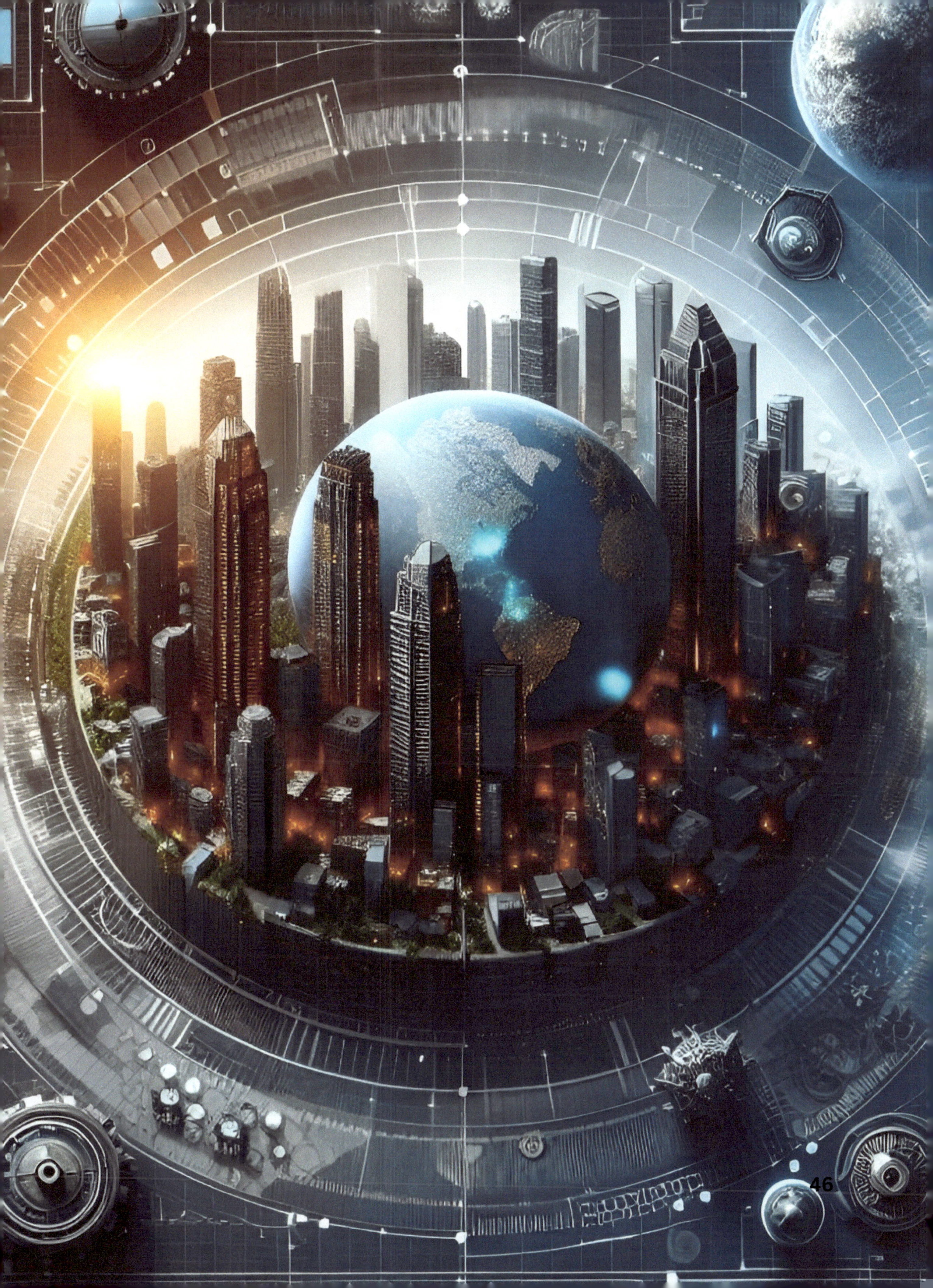

The political landscape of Guyana is characterized by a history of diverse governance systems and occasional challenges, including periods of authoritarian rule and democratic reforms.

Recent years have seen significant political developments, such as the resolution of longstanding electoral disputes and efforts to strengthen democratic institutions.

The population's engagement in electoral processes reflects a commitment to democratic principles and governance reforms aimed at enhancing transparency and accountability.

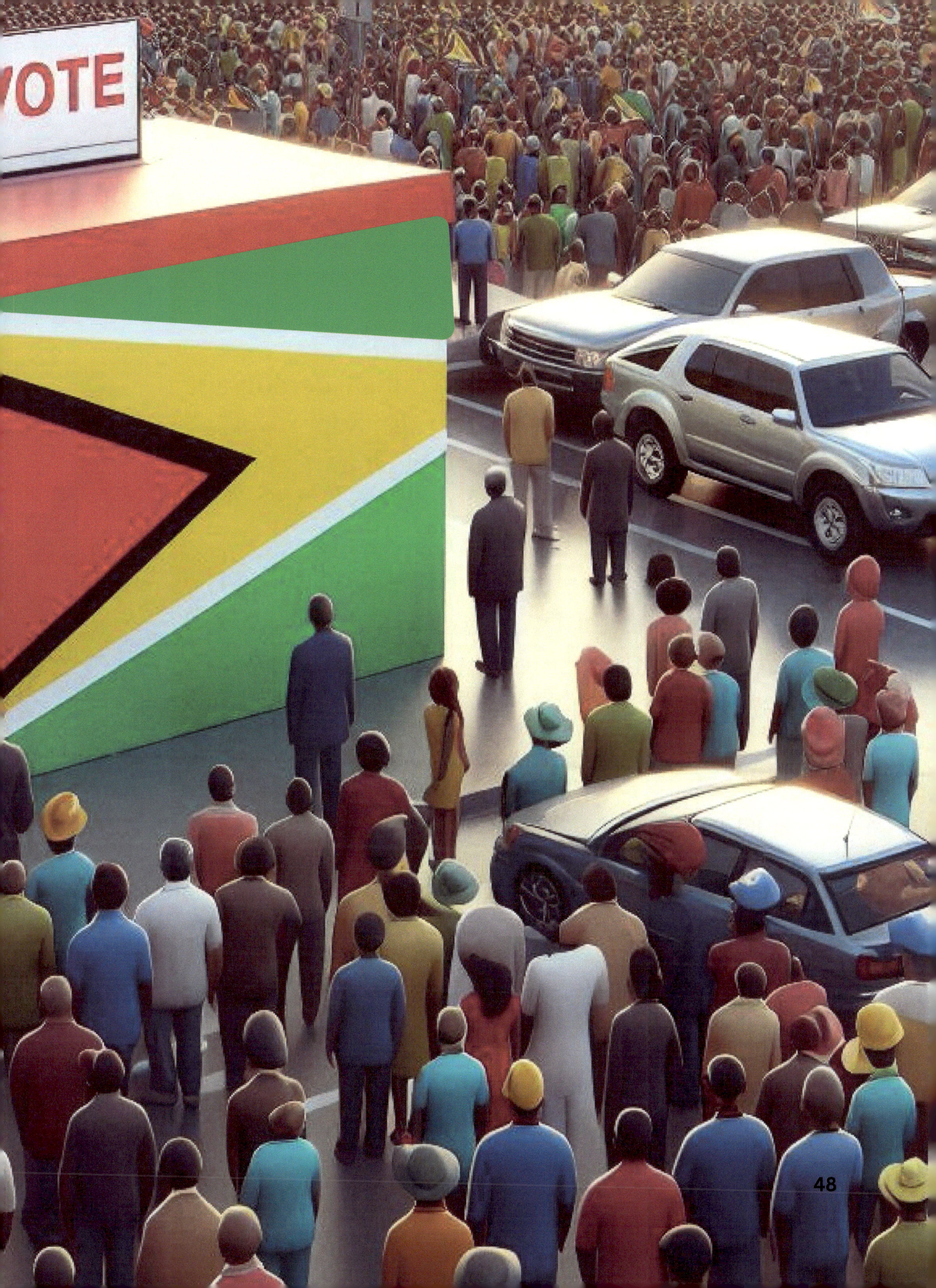
VOTE

Guyana's youth represent a critical demographic shaping the nation's future, with opportunities and challenges in education, employment, and civic engagement.

 Initiatives promoting youth empowerment through education and skills development are essential for harnessing their potential as future leaders and innovators.

Addressing issues such as youth unemployment and ensuring inclusive access to education are crucial steps towards building a vibrant and sustainable future for Guyana.

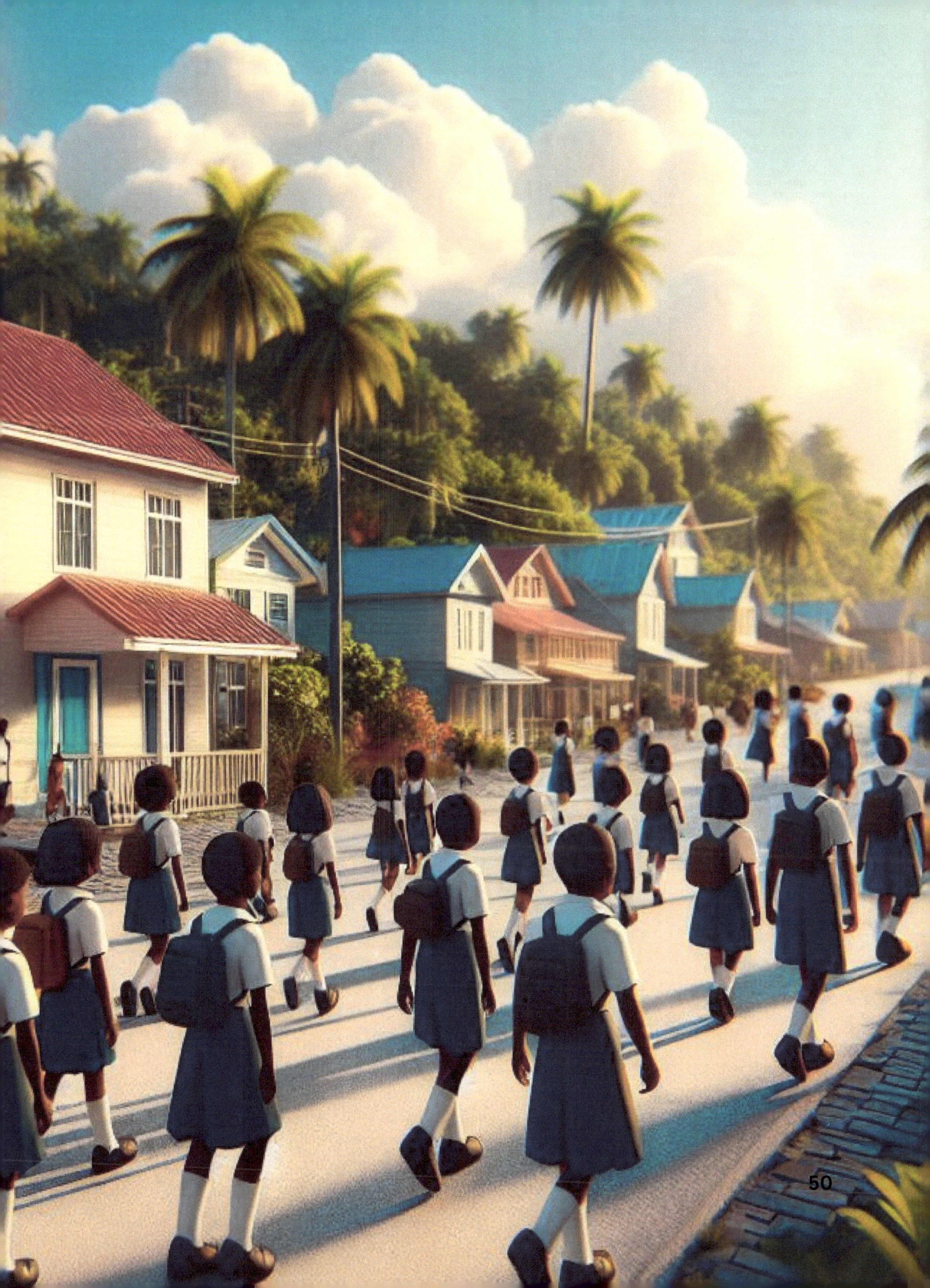

Chapter 9: Some of the Highlights of Guyana

Kaieteur Falls: One of the world's most powerful waterfalls; it is situated on the Potaro River in the Kaieteur National Park, which is in the Amazon rainforest.

Kaieteur Falls has a single drop of about 226 meters (741 feet), making it one of the tallest waterfalls in the world when considering its uninterrupted drop. It also has a width of approximately 113 meters (370 feet). In terms of volume, it is notable for its forceful flow.

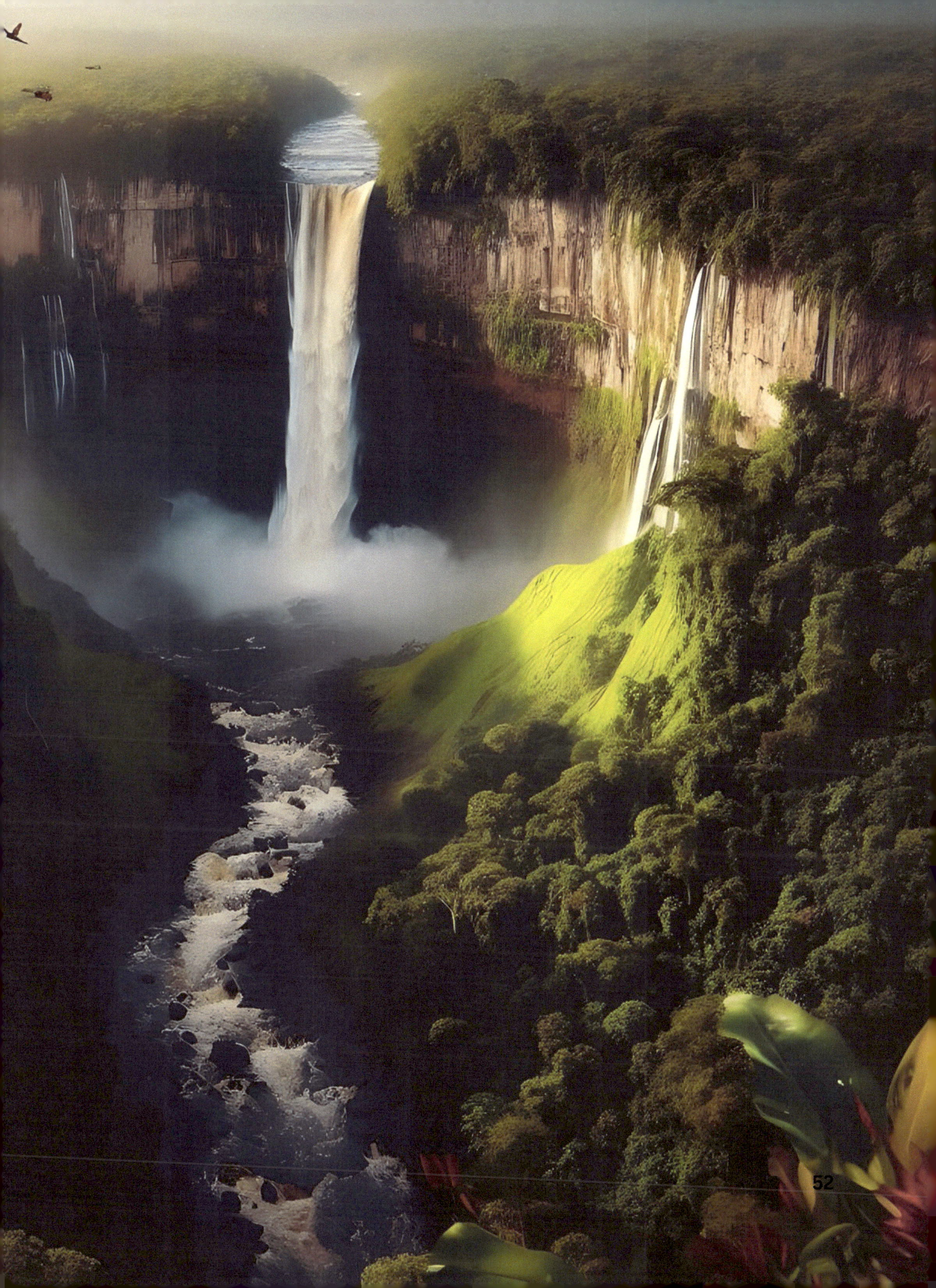

Stabroek Market: A bustling market in Georgetown, offering a vibrant display of local produce, crafts, and daily life.

Stabroek Market is situated along the western bank of the Demerara River, in the heart of Georgetown, Guyana's largest city and capital.

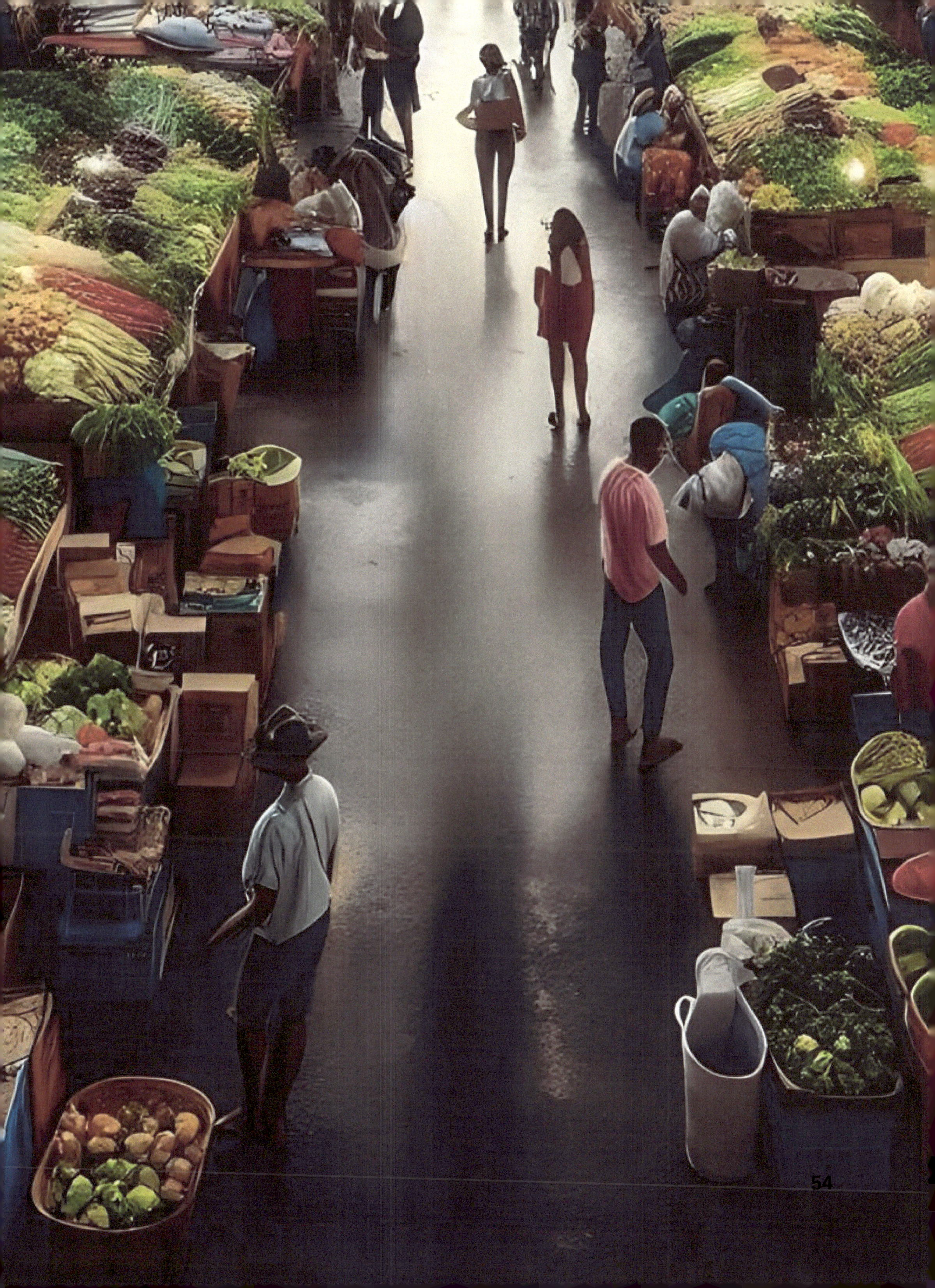

Demerara Harbour Bridge: The longest floating bridge in the world, connecting Georgetown to the western bank of the Demerara River.

The total length of the bridge is approximately 1.8 kilometers (1.1 miles), making it one of the longest floating bridges in the world. The bridge can open and close to allow large ships and vessels to pass through the Demerara River.

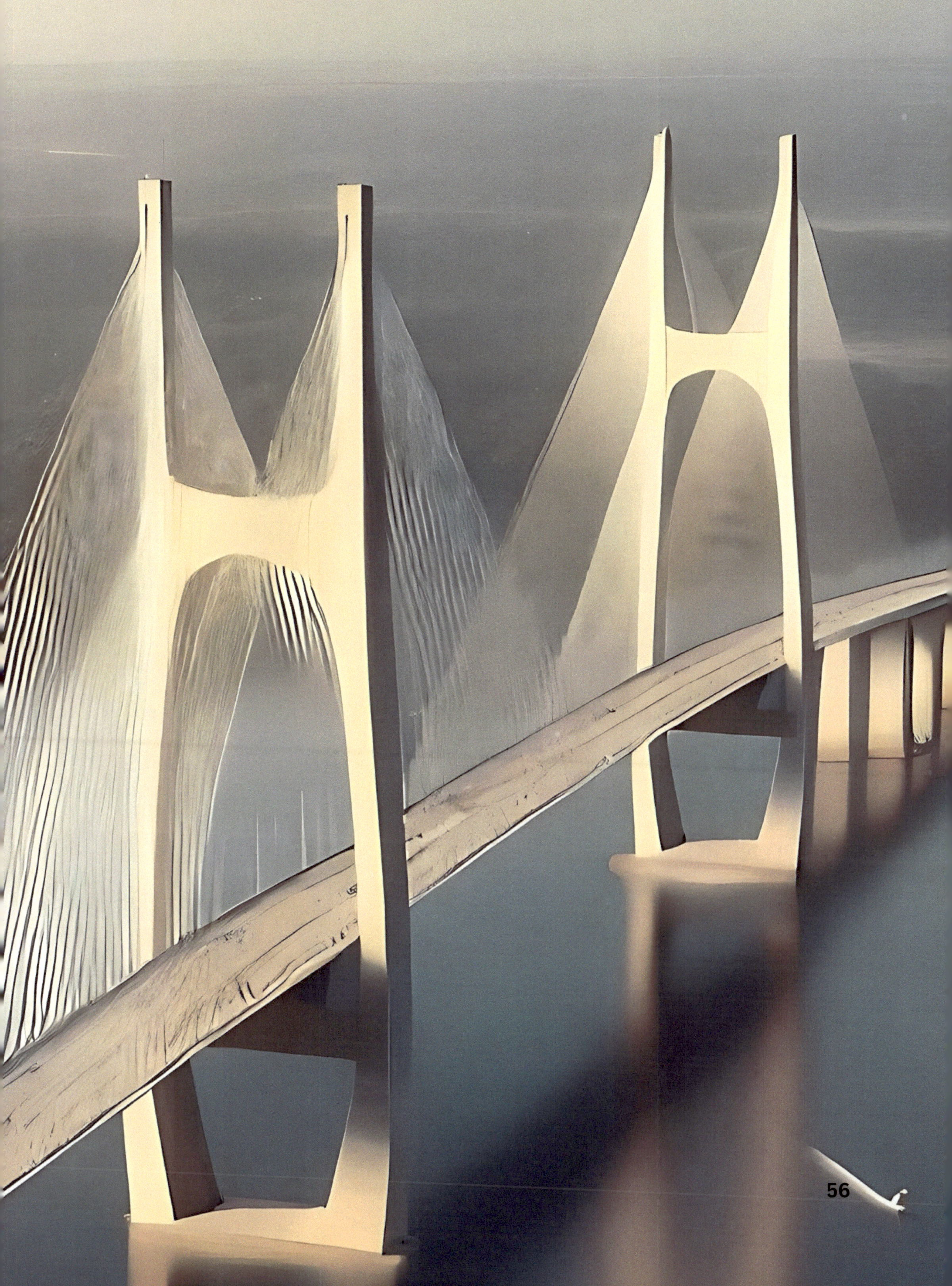

Guyanese Rum: Renowned for its rich flavor and quality, including brands like El Dorado Rum, produced from Demerara sugar where many of the country's sugarcane plantations historically thrived. Demerara rum is characterized by its deep, complex flavors with notes of caramel, molasses, and tropical spices.

Guyanese rum has gained international acclaim and is highly regarded among rum enthusiasts and connoisseurs. Its rich history, traditional production methods, and distinctive flavors have contributed to its popularity on the global stage.

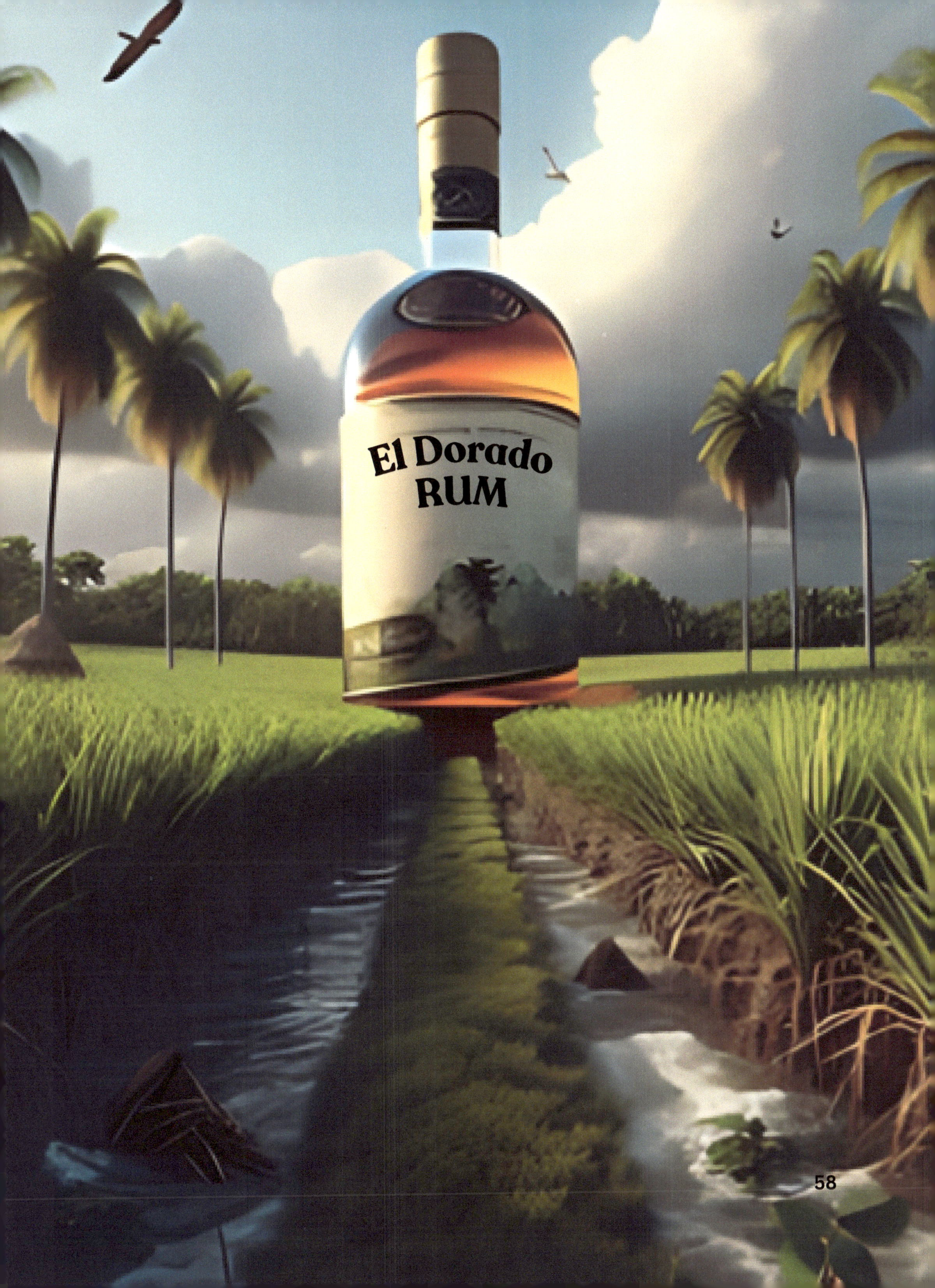

El Dorado
RUM

Georgetown's Wooden Architecture: Colonial-era buildings and cathedrals like St. George's Cathedral, made entirely from wood.

Much of Georgetown's wooden architecture dates back to the 18th and 19th centuries, influenced by Dutch, British, and French colonial styles. These colonial powers left their architectural imprint on the city, shaping its distinctive character.

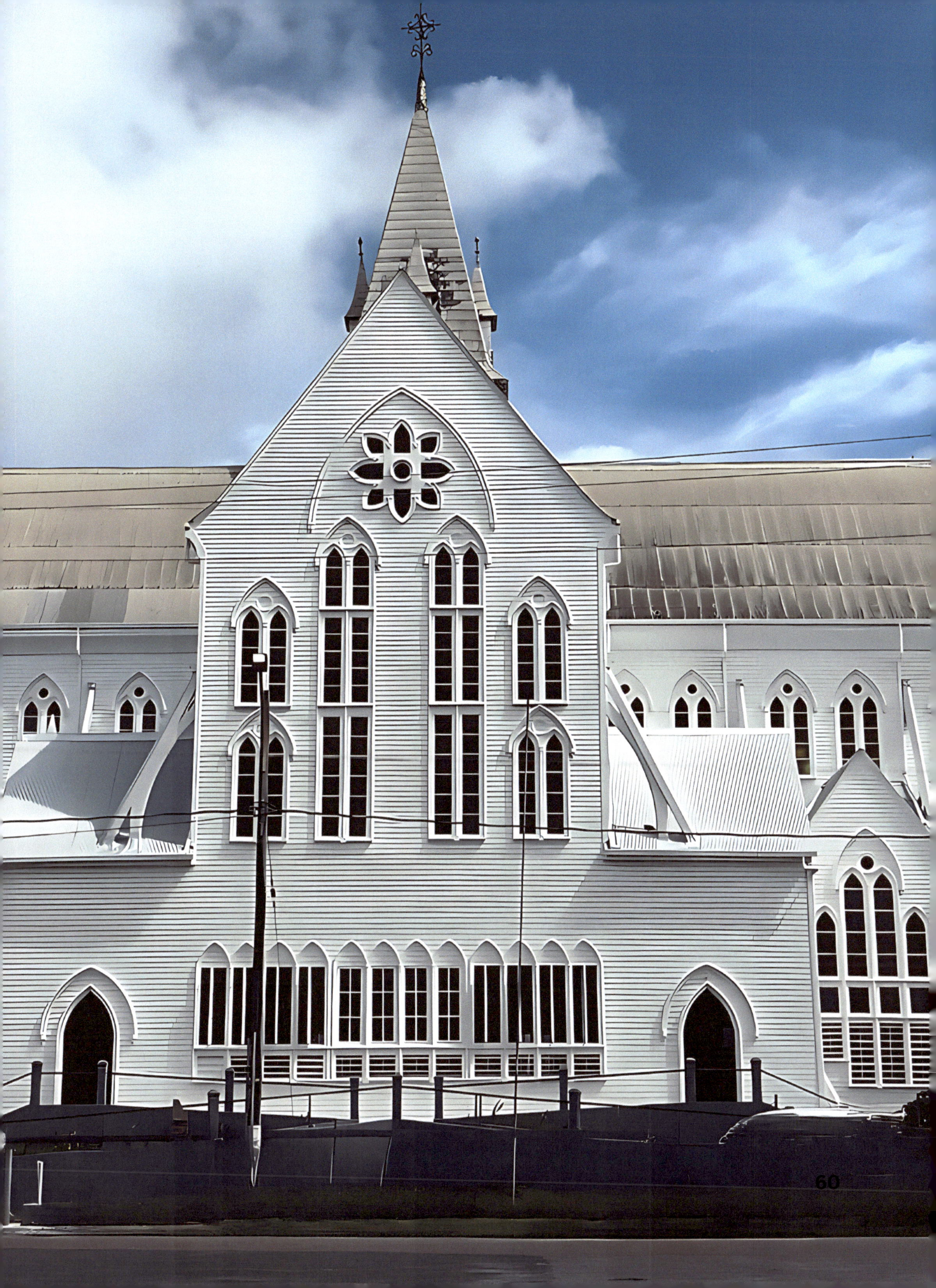

Guyanese Cricket: A national passion with local leagues and international matches held at venues like the Providence Stadium.

Cricket has been played in Guyana since the 18th century, introduced by British colonizers. It quickly became immensely popular among both the elite and working classes, transcending social barriers.

Guyana has produced many legendary cricketers who have made significant contributions to West Indies cricket. Players like Clive Lloyd, Rohan Kanhai, Lance Gibbs, Alvin Kallicharran, and Shivnarine Chanderpaul are among the most illustrious names who have represented the West Indies with distinction.

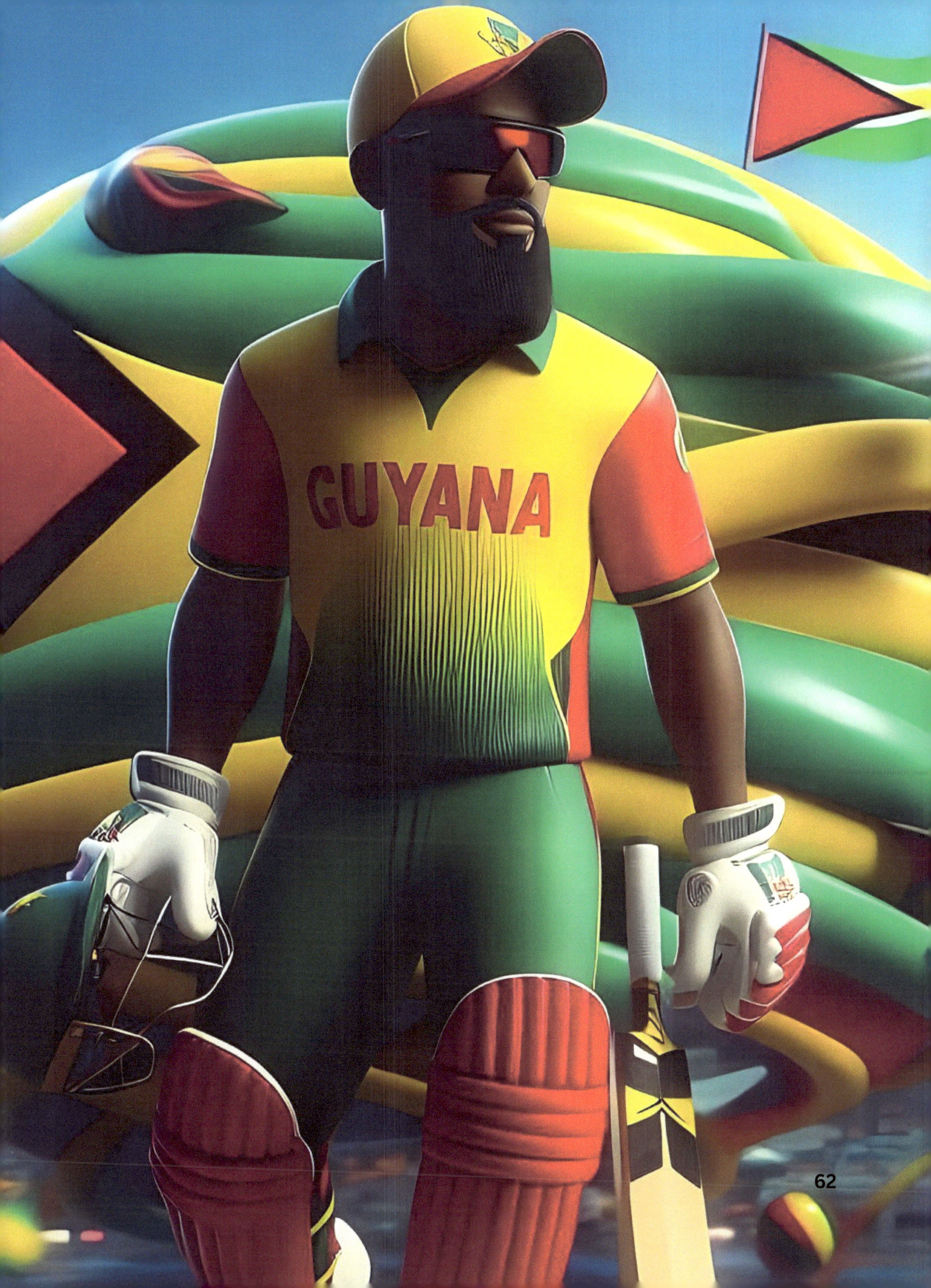
GUYANA

Jaguar and Giant River Otter: Iconic and charismatic animals found in the Amazon rainforest, including parts of Guyana.

Jaguars (Panthera onca) are the largest big cats native to the Americas and are found in a variety of habitats, including rainforests, grasslands, and swamps. They are particularly associated with dense tropical forests like those found in Guyana

The giant river otter (Pteronura brasiliensis) is found in the rivers and lakes of the Amazon basin, including those in Guyana. They prefer slow-moving rivers, oxbow lakes, and flooded forests.

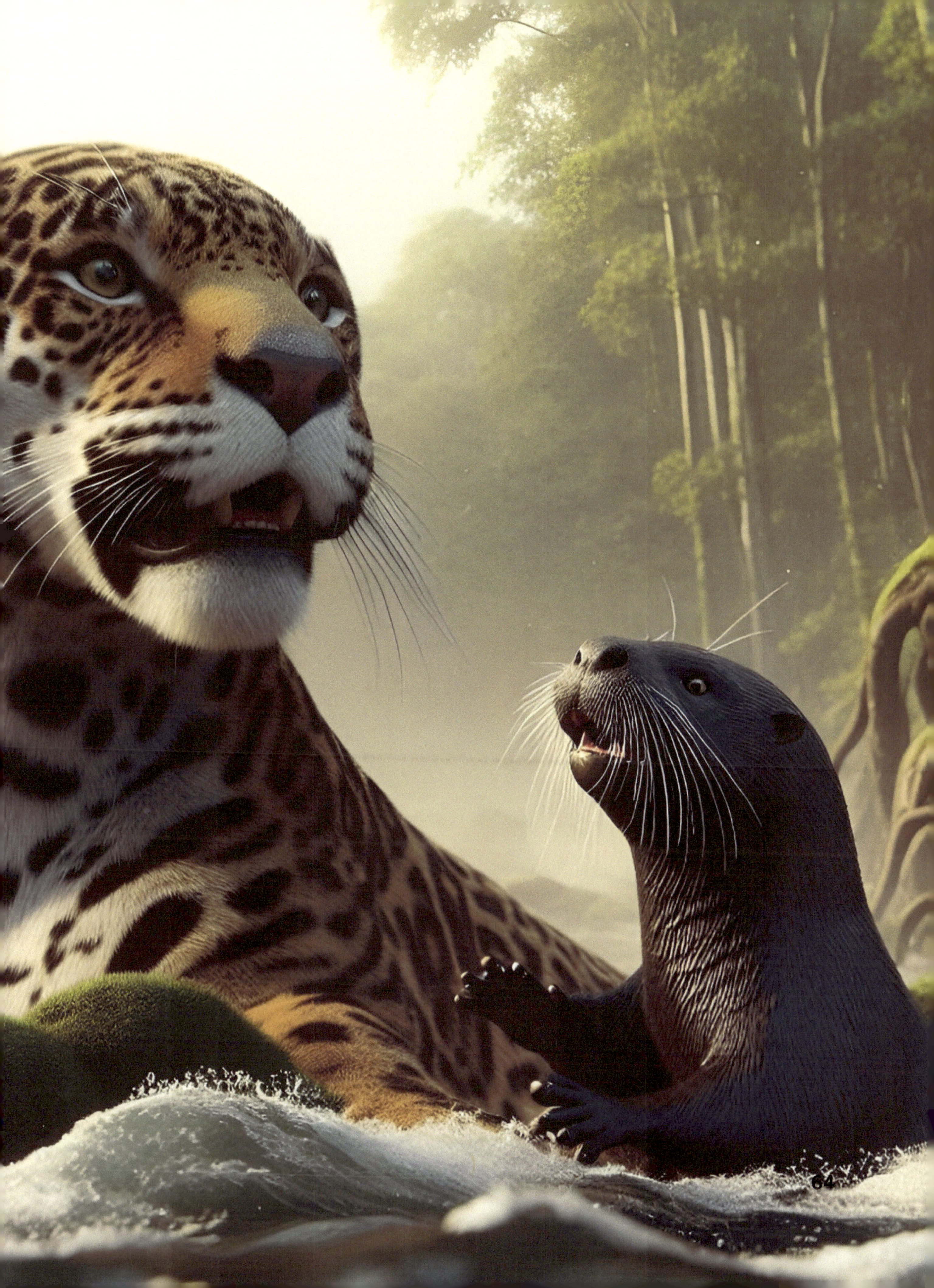

Shell Beach: Along Guyana's coastline, a sanctuary for endangered sea turtles during nesting season. It is located in the northwest part of Guyana, in Region 1, stretching over 120 km (75 miles) of beach and mudflats.

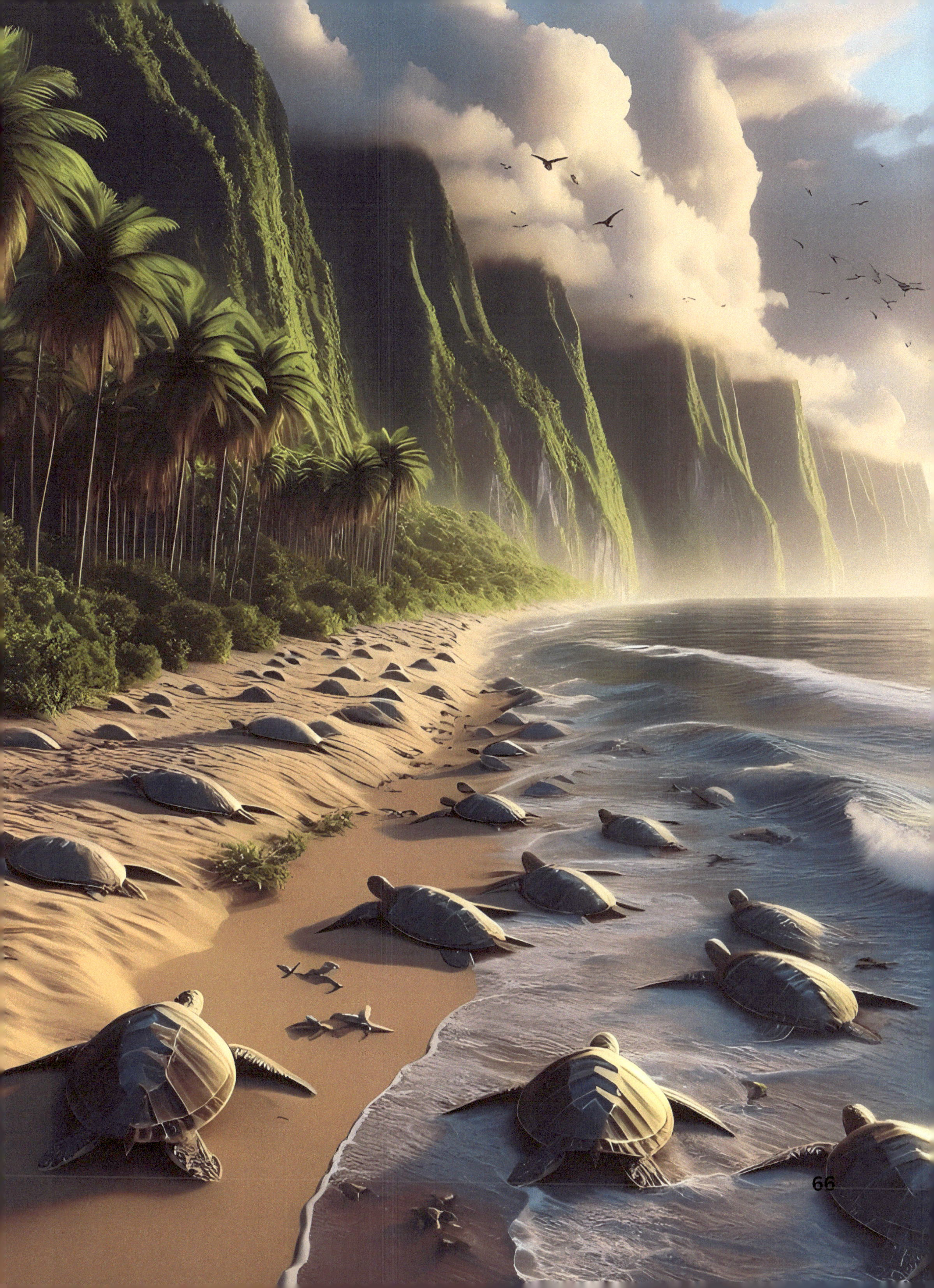

Iwokrama Forest: A protected area known for its biodiversity and research station, promoting sustainable development and conservation. It is located in the heart of the <u>Guiana Shield</u>, one of the four last pristine tropical forests in the world.

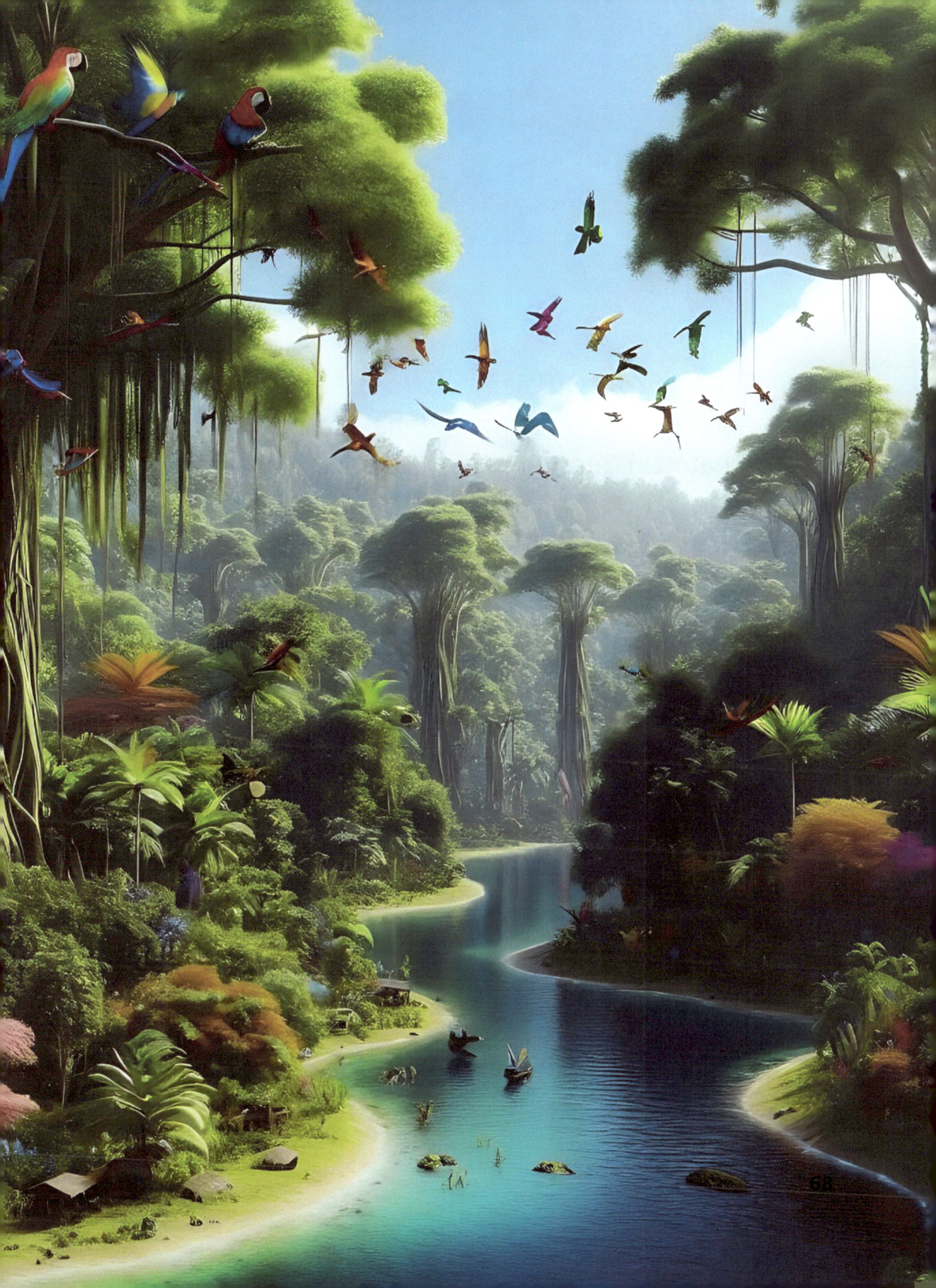

Guyana Zoo: Officially known as the Guyana Zoological Park, is the national zoo of Guyana, located in Georgetown, the capital city.

The zoo was established in 1952 and has since served as a center for wildlife conservation, education, and public recreation.

The Guyana Zoo is home to a variety of native and exotic species of animals, including mammals, birds, reptiles, and fish. Some of the notable species include jaguars, tapirs, giant river otters, monkeys, toucans, macaws, and various reptiles such as snakes and turtles.

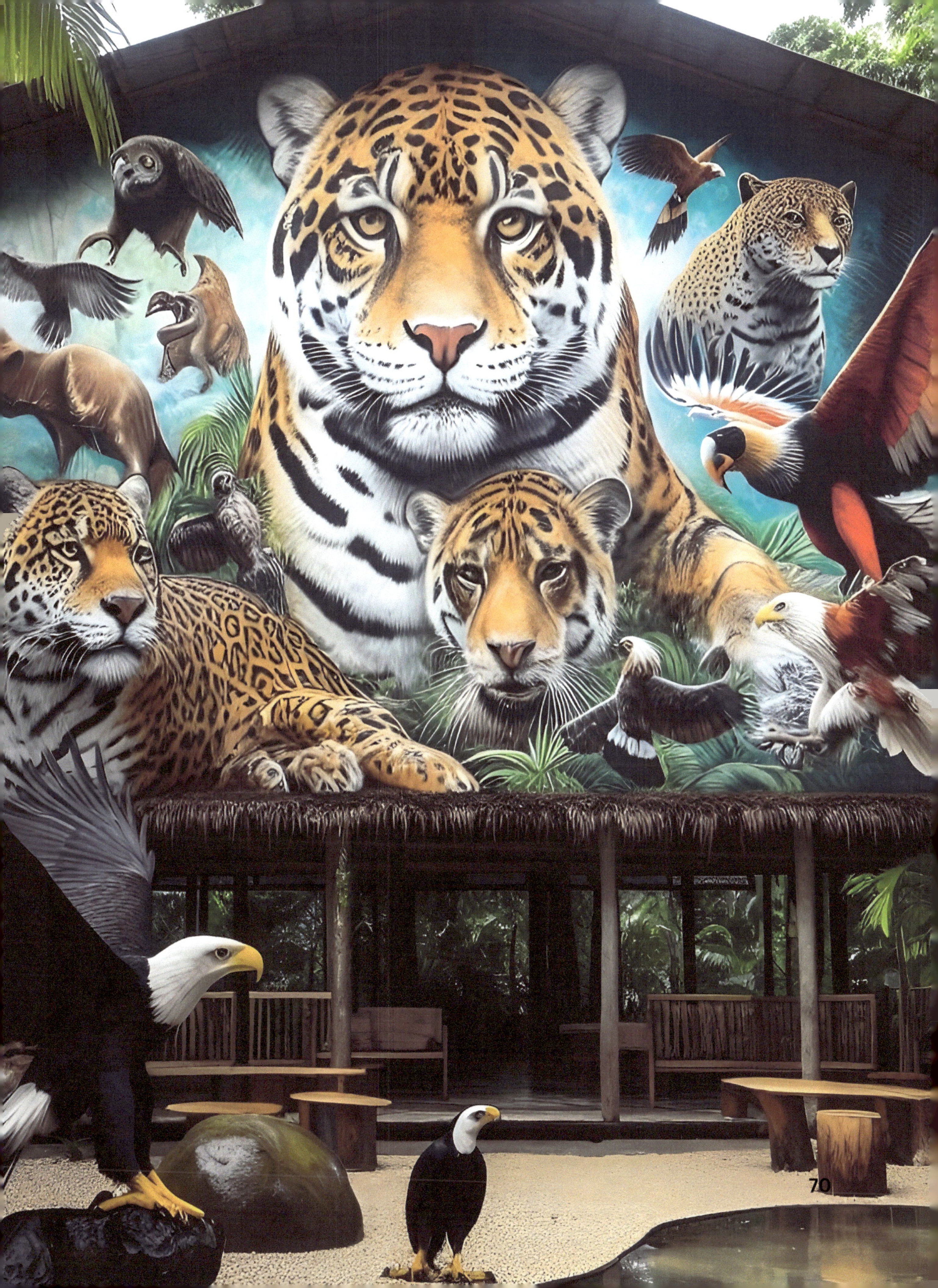

Guyana is divided into 10 administrative regions:

Barima-Waini (Region 1)
Pomeroon-Supenaam (Region 2)
Essequibo Islands-West Demerara (Region 3)
Demerara-Mahaica (Region 4)
Mahaica-Berbice (Region 5)
East Berbice-Corentyne (Region 6)
Cuyuni-Mazaruni (Region 7)
Potaro-Siparuni (Region 8)
Upper Takutu-Upper Essequibo (Region 9)
Upper Demerara-Berbice (Region 10)

Each region is further subdivided into smaller administrative units known as Neighbourhood Democratic Councils (NDCs) or Municipalities, depending on urban or rural classification. These regions play a significant role in local governance, infrastructure development, and service delivery across Guyana.

The past eight presidents of Guyana, spanning from the country's independence in 1966 to the present:

Sir Arthur Chung (1970-1980) - Guyana's first President after it became a republic in 1970.

Forbes Burnham (1980-1985) - Elected as the first Executive President after Guyana became a republic. He served until his death in 1985.

Desmond Hoyte (1985-1992) - Succeeded Forbes Burnham and oversaw the transition to democratic governance.

Cheddi Jagan (1992-1997) - Won Guyana's first democratic elections after years of socialist rule.

Sam Hinds (1997-1999, 2001-2015) - Acted as President on two occasions and served as Prime Minister for many years.

Bharrat Jagdeo (1999-2011) - Succeeded Sam Hinds and focused on economic development during his presidency.

Donald Ramotar (2011-2015) - Elected as President and focused on social policies and infrastructure development.

David A. Granger (2015-2020) - Elected President in 2015 and focused on national unity, security, and development.

Mohamed Irfaan Ali (2020-present) - Elected President in 2020 following a contentious election period. His presidency is focused on economic recovery, infrastructure development, and environmental sustainability.

In conclusion, Guyana stands as a testament to the richness of cultural diversity and natural beauty nestled within South America. From its indigenous roots to the influences of colonialism and migration, the nation has forged a unique identity shaped by a tapestry of traditions, languages, and culinary delights. As Guyana navigates modern challenges and embraces future opportunities, its strength lies in the unity of its people and the resilience of its cultural heritage, promising a vibrant future rooted in a deep appreciation for its past.

ONE PEOPLE

ONE NATION

ONE DESTINY